THE MIGRANT CHEF

ALSO BY LAURA TILLMAN

The Long Shadow of Small Ghosts:
Murder and Memory in an American City

THE
MIGRANT
CHEF

୬

The Life and Times of
Lalo García

LAURA TILLMAN

W. W. NORTON & COMPANY
Celebrating a Century of Independent Publishing

For information about permission to reproduce selections from this book, write to
Permissions, W. W. Norton & Company, Inc., 500 Fifth Avenue, New York, NY 10110

For information about special discounts for bulk purchases, please contact
W. W. Norton Special Sales at specialsales@wwnorton.com or 800-233-4830

Manufacturing by Lake Book Manufacturing
Book design by Patrice Sheridan
Production manager: Julia Druskin

ISBN: 978-1-324-00577-3

W. W. Norton & Company, Inc.
500 Fifth Avenue, New York, N.Y. 10110
www.wwnorton.com

W. W. Norton & Company Ltd.
15 Carlisle Street, London W1D 3BS

1 2 3 4 5 6 7 8 9 0

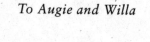

To Augie and Willa

CONTENTS

AUTHOR'S NOTE

THIS BOOK IS the result of five years of reporting. This includes hundreds of hours in the kitchen of Máximo Bistrot, observing and conducting interviews with Eduardo "Lalo" García Guzmán, the staff of the kitchen and dining room, the purveyors and customers; interviews with chefs and staff of other fine dining restaurants in Mexico City, including historically significant restaurants that have since shuttered; three weeks working in the pastry kitchen of Rosetta; reporting trips to Guanajuato, the Estado de México, Baja California, Dubai, Salinas, California, and Georgia, with stops in Atlanta, Uvalda and Vidalia, all of which were funded independently; and interviews with Lalo's former employers, coworkers, friends, and family members.

I interviewed dozens of experts about issues that relate to Lalo's experiences, including Mexico's gastronomic history, migrant farm labor, the impact of the North American Free Trade Agreement, restaurant criticism, pesticide exposure, U.S. and Mexican political history as it pertains to immigration and enforcement, sustainable agriculture, labor law, and Mexico City's contemporary fine dining movement. Whenever possible, I interviewed primary sources and visited the environments significant to Lalo's story in an attempt to better understand his life, gather additional detail, and verify information. I read extensively on all of these topics, including anthropological, historical, and sociological works from scholars, memoirs and essays by contemporaries, police and immigration records, and literary works. When Lalo's inner world is described, the details included in the text are the result of extensive conversations with him about his emotional life, his reaction to events, and follow-up conversations about what he was thinking and feeling during specific moments. Many of those reactions ran counter to what I might have imagined, and Lalo's willingness to be candid and patient was critical to this process. A note on translation: I am conversationally fluent in Spanish. Whenever possible I recorded interviews to ensure accurate quotes and translations. Lalo, who today is fluent in English, is most often quoted without the need for translation.

Much of Lalo's work as a chef has been documented in some form. Awards, openings, controversies, and closings have all found a place in the public record, and it's been relatively easy to verify names, dates, and other information related to his successful career as a chef and restaurateur. However, there is scant documentation available of his early life, and his memory of that time is imperfect. I've been able to verify some information by visiting Lalo's former homes in the Estado de México and Guanajuato, interviewing family members and friends, viewing family photos, and cross-checking details, like those regarding pesticide exposure and migrant labor, with experts. When it was not possible to verify a date or piece of important information, Lalo's family members generously spent their time comparing recollections to reach consensus. Areas in which there is uncertainty have been documented in the endnotes.

I met Lalo in 2016. When I phoned Máximo Bistrot for an interview with its chef, I had no idea that Lalo was at a critical moment in his life: Mexican immigrants were increasingly being used as political pawns during the U.S. presidential election, and Lalo wanted to share his story. He did so through various interviews with the media during the course of that year, but he wanted someone to take it on in greater depth. I'd called Máximo Bistrot because I was interested in the possibility of writing about the cooks, waiters, dishwashers, and purveyors who worked in a fine dining restaurant in Mexico City, where the country's extreme inequalities are both reinforced and questioned. When I met Lalo, I understood that his journey had pushed him to contend with these forces over and over again.

I've done my best to tell his story with the accuracy and rigor of a journalist, supported by the research discussed above; there were no constraints on my inquiry. Lalo granted me extraordinary access to the life of his restaurant—whether it was a calm morning before service or a hectic dinner rush, I was able to freely observe, interview, and take notes. Lalo has also participated in an ongoing dialogue with me about not only what has happened in his life, but what these events have meant to him. I'm grateful for his commitment, his vulnerability, and all I've learned from him. I hope readers will be able to share in that experience.

PROLOGUE

ONE MORNING IN October of 2016, a young woman walked to the corner of Tonalá and Zacatecas in Mexico City, toward a restaurant with a simple black awning. Its white lettering read, *Máximo Bistrot Local*. She had been enrolled in a vocational cooking program and had come to Máximo in search of a job. If successful, she would join millions of local service workers who undertake hours-long commutes daily: the walk to a street corner and the wait for a dingy van, the crouched shuffle inside the door to sardine next to passengers smelling of their morning coffee and spritz of perfume, or the sweat and Fabuloso still clinging to the uniform from yesterday's shift. When they are dropped at a metro stop, the descent past *tamal* vendors into the tunnels carved through the muddy foundation of this ancient metropolis, its canals once pulsing with lake water, now drained. The Valley of Mexico is ringed by snow-capped mountains, volcanos that trap pollution and seem to volley the sounds of 22 million inhabitants—the clang of the garbage collector's bell and the barking dog, the operatic call of *"el gaaaaasssss,"* the prerecorded vendor hawking avocados and guavas. Finally, up, up, up from the metro and into the streets of the well-to-do neighborhood of the Colonia Roma, with its turn-of-the-century mansions converted into cafés and apartments, its tidy parks with fountains and purebred dogs fetching for their masters.

On this day, the young woman walked through the doorway toward the marble counter where Chef Eduardo García Guzmán, known to most everyone here as Lalo, prepared the day's menu, which changed with the seasons and his whims. Though the men in his family were blessed with thick manes that lasted into old age, five years of running the restaurant had pilfered the hairs from the top of his head.

At first glance, he didn't look the part of a famous restaurant owner: his shirt was usually stained, and he could often be found performing the most menial tasks in the kitchen, like sorting through mushrooms or scaling fish. But authority radiated from his eyes, framed by arched brows; the rest of the staff shifted around him, a school of minnows darting back from a larger specimen. Those eyes were always asking questions, protecting against hidden motives, searching for signs of true passion.

Lalo walked out from behind the counter, wiped his hands on a rag, and led the job applicant to the best table in the restaurant, a disc of dark tropical hardwood in a cozy alcove facing an open doorway, crowded with olive trees in terra-cotta pots. She had been enrolled in Gastromotiva, a foundation that helps Mexico's economically vulnerable to get the training they need to obtain well-paying kitchen jobs. Lalo fundraised for the program and welcomed its participants for job interviews like this one.

The first thing she needed to do, he said, was come in for a test shift.

"We want you to see how we work—because it's tough," he told her, his body relaxed, his gaze intent. "The profession you've chosen is one of the most difficult, but once you embrace it and you overcome the initial barrier, it's one of the best in the world."

He asked where she lived—not to gossip, he assured her, but because she'd be working twelve-hour days, and he knew the commute could turn that into fifteen or sixteen. He'd try to accommodate her if he could.

"The fact is, where you live, there aren't restaurants where you can work, because on the one hand they can't pay you well, and, on the other, you can't learn from the people that work there. So, you made a good decision by coming here. But then again, maybe not. Maybe it's too far away. That's life, that's the reality."

If she didn't take the time to learn now, her career would flatline, he warned.

"Listen, I'm more sincere than the rest," he said. "I'm not going to sell you the clouds because that's not how this business works. If you learn the business, you can achieve something incredible, but first you need to commit totally. First, you'll have to give it your best try."

Gracias, she said. Lalo called over his assistant to help her schedule a date for a trial shift; normally she'd begin at 6 a.m., but she could come in at 7 if she needed to. Then he went back to work, unsure if his candid talk about the grueling nature of the business would ultimately intimidate or inspire. She never came back. As with so many others, Lalo never bothered to learn her name.

People sought Lalo out constantly. From the dairy farmer who came to the city to convince Lalo to put his queso fresco on the menu, to the preening millennial millionaire eager to add him to his circle of friends, they walked through the door day after day. Lalo was now one of the most famous chefs in Mexico, his flagship restau-

rant a destination for tourists from around the world, named one of
the fifty best in Latin America, the best in Mexico. He'd developed a
reputation as a man who would hear you out and try to help—if the
request had merit. He wasn't the country's most famous or influential
chef—that title belonged to his mentor, Enrique Olvera, of the restaurant Pujol—but he was the one people came to as a confidant, the
one you didn't need an appointment to see. A stranger might walk
into the restaurant, and, if the cause was worthy, Lalo would do more
than give them the shirt off his back. He'd open his closet and give
away every shirt he owned. But if he didn't approve, he'd nod non-
committally, say the idea was "amazing," and never return their calls.

Among his employees in the crowded galley kitchen, he could be
a cook's best ally; in his mind, this also meant being their harshest
critic. Without his high standards, how could he propel these young
hopefuls, how could he help them turn another service industry job
into a career—and an opportunity to ascend into the country's fragile middle class? Lalo could hold out his hand and pull people out of
poverty if they were willing to put in the work, but he was frustrated
daily, disillusioned by lack of commitment, worried that every time
he stepped away, the train would run off the track.

Enrique Olvera was known for his innovative spirit: he could
deconstruct and reconstruct traditional concepts, creating something that bore his distinct signature, starting trends that trickled
through mid-market eateries and into home kitchens, spreading
ideas that drew people close to an unfamiliar culture. Lalo had traveled tens of thousands of miles to eat at such restaurants, like the out-
post at the end of a Scandinavian road, course after course composed
of moss and foraged herbs and cured reindeer. Food that required
thousands of dollars for planes and taxis and hotel rooms before you
even got the check. This food interested him, sure. Lalo had happily

taken those journeys, and had found inspiration at the end of the rainbow. But he couldn't seem to entirely suspend his conscience, to enjoy without being reminded of the nauseating math of excess and famine. "There are people who can't even get a clean glass of water, it's fucked up. How do you wrap your mind around it? You don't. If you do, you just become miserable." Lalo had no desire to craft forms of privilege so esoteric that most people were unaware they even existed.

Sometimes, he daydreamed about a future when the world economy would crash, the tourists would stop coming, and he could close his restaurants and go back to the village where he was born. He'd build a house with his hands. He'd raise cows and pigs and make his own cheese and charcuterie. He'd sleep under the stars and wake up with the sun. Then there were days when he could envision the contours of an empire: a dozen restaurants, providing a livelihood for a thousand people. A presidency where he'd make his first act the construction of an enormous prison where he could lock up the narcos and politicians who were ruining his country. As he cooked, Lalo talked to his staff and his wife about what he'd seen on the news and what ought to be done about it. But when people praised him for the jobs he created or his environmental work, he grew stoic, the expression drained from his face, and he said things like, "I'm just a simple cook who feeds people who are hungry."

Lalo had worked for success—at times defined simply as survival—since he was a lanky ten-year-old, picking oranges and digging onions on the route from Florida to Michigan. Now, the small bistro he had opened with his wife, Gaby, had blossomed into three restaurants they owned and several others they advised. Máximo Bistrot had become a meeting point for the wealthy and powerful; when he shook hands with well-heeled businessmen and long-limbed tourists, he was there but not there, stealing distracted moments to return to the oasis of his village, an idealized version that consisted of woodsmoke and starlight. But in his waking life, when he made that trip, he couldn't stand himself: a rich man driving into a poor town that barely knew him.

The choices and demands he made each day masked deep-seated anxieties. Yes, this was assuredly the right sauce for this entrée, the wrong chef de partie for this job. But were the people who surrounded him compadres, or a series of well-disguised parasites, gently draining his blood as they smiled? Was this life of "hospitality," where money and kind gestures commingled to vertiginous effect, leading him astray?

When Lalo declared himself a "simple cook who feeds people who are hungry," he knew that, in fact, his interior and exterior life increasingly had grown complex. That the people who came to his restaurants expected an experience that transcended hunger. That the closer he got to the next goalpost, the further a pat ideal like "happiness" or "success" retreated from view. In its pursuit, what would he finally gain? What would he lose that couldn't be bought back?

THE MIGRANT CHEF

Natalia and Lalo in San José de las Pilas

Courtesy of the García family

CHAPTER ONE

TORTILLAS AT DAWN

LALO WAS BORN in 1977, brought home from a rural clinic to the village of San José de las Pilas, Guanajuato, in central Mexico, a community so small it doesn't appear on a state map. There, most families grew the fruits and vegetables in their primarily vegetarian diet, along with corn and sorghum to sell at market. To earn more, you had to leave, a message that was reinforced by continuous departures. That exodus included Lalo's uncles, who moved from Guanajuato to the growing city of Nicolás Romero in the Estado de México, which hugs Mexico City on three sides. There, they built homes and got jobs in a Ray-O-Vac battery factory.

The family was part of a massive migration from Guanajuato, Puebla, and Guerrero to the Estado de México, which saw its population double in the 1970s, reaching 7.5 million people by the end of the decade. Millions of newcomers were attracted by affordable land, and job opportunities in Mexico City, within commuting distance. There, they staffed kitchens, cleaned homes, worked construction, waited on tables, drove taxis, and cared for children, contributing to the service economy that kept Mexico City's middle and upper classes looked after.

Lalo's father, Lupe, began migrating to the United States to pick fruit and vegetables shortly after he married Lalo's mother, Natalia. Lupe returned to Mexico very occasionally, sometimes for a week or a month at a time, when the harvest schedule slowed. On those visits, the couple reacquainted themselves, eventually bringing four children into the world: Maria, Isela, Lalo, and Jaime. About a year after Jaime, the youngest, was born, Lupe returned to the village to move his family to a plot of land next to his brother's new home in the Estado de México. He tried joining his brothers in the Ray-O-Vac plant, but, having spent his whole working life outdoors, he felt confined by the bleak factory and frustrated with the paltry hourly wage. At least in the fields, there was always the possibility of filling more buckets in the pursuit of a fatter billfold. He returned to the migrant route.

Natalia pinched every peso that Lupe sent back to fund concrete block and rebar for their new home. At first, they lived in a single room with a dirt floor, a curtain blowing in the doorframe. For a bathroom, they'd visit one of the adjacent fields. Between the house and the alley there was a sinkhole, and when it rained—as it did six or seven months of the year on a daily basis—they jury-rigged a bridge of wood planks across the quickly-forming pond. In the years that followed they would slowly add more rooms: a second room where Natalia could cook and where some of them would sleep. Another room became a living area, and later, a place for Lalo's aunt Camelia, a nun, to live.

When the team of construction workers came by to pour the concrete for a new room, Natalia rounded up one of their pigs and Lalo's uncle would come by to perform the slaughter—raising the hog's front hoof and then stabbing it in the heart. Natalia drained the blood and butchered the meat, then sold some cuts and saved some to make carnitas. She boiled the blood with onion and folded this loose black sausage into tacos to feed the construction crew. This dish, *moronga*, was one of Lalo's first favorite delicacies.

Eating moronga signified that the family had made it a little further toward a discernible goal. A house was something you could touch, and Natalia loved their half-made home in the Estado de México tenderly. She knew the painstaking origins of every concrete block. When the house was finally completed, its walls formed a square around a central courtyard where Natalia cultivated chayote, figs, and roses.

During one of Lupe's trips back, a scrawny Lalo did his best to help his father with the job of filling the sinkhole with truckloads of dirt until they had created a level yard outside their doorway. Later, when the neighborhood had grown up around them and become dense and dodgy, they erected a gray concrete wall, unabashedly utilitarian, with excess rebar reaching skyward in case they decided to build it higher one day.

For more than a decade, Natalia raised the kids with the money Lupe sent back from his work in the fields. Sometimes the payments got waylaid or lost, and she'd have to beg the neighbors for food. Sometimes a three-foot-tall Lalo went out looking for work. He moved bricks for a one-man factory in the neighborhood; he tended to the pigs that belonged to his sister's schoolteacher, Maestro Chon. Lalo came home with gifts of ice cream for the family, purchased with his earnings. Natalia told him the work was too dangerous, but Lalo insisted: he didn't want his siblings to miss out on anything.

In an early photograph of the Garcías in the Estado de México, they're dwarfed by the mature cornstalks that surrounded their home. Soon, urban sprawl would make the memory of those fields seem like nothing more than a hallucination. For the neighborhood's residents, what had been reasonable distances between home and work in the capital became choked with traffic, and free hours during the standard Monday-through-Saturday workweek slipped away, consumed by the journey.

In the summers, Lalo traveled with his mother and siblings back to San José de las Pilas, a hamlet two dozen shades of green hugging a hillside, overlooking a swell of mountains, to help his grandparents work the fields. They celebrated Lalo's arrival by preparing his favorite foods: *tamales de ceniza*—ash-infused corn masa steamed inside a recently-picked green corn leaf, served with fresh tomato salsa on top—and grilled goat. When they returned every September to the Estado de México, each time more urban than the last, Lalo grew claustrophobic and went into mourning for his life in the country, weepily shuffling around the house as Natalia grew frustrated with his theatrics.

So when Lupe came back to Mexico intent on convincing Natalia that she should bring the boys, now ten and eight, across the border—that they were ready to make the trip and lend a hand in the fields—Lalo was game. Natalia was harder to persuade: she knew that the migrant lifestyle was too dangerous for their daughters Isela and Maria, and leaving Mexico would mean leaving them behind. Even after Natalia agreed, it took days to finally depart: each time they made an attempt, the family would mourn the impending separation so tearfully, so intolerably, that they'd throw up their hands and decide to stay just a little longer. Finally, in the middle of the night, they boarded the first in a series of buses that would take them to Tijuana. The entry point was far from Lupe's routine work in Florida, but he decided that Tijuana's comparatively urban terrain would be safer for the children to traverse than the vast Sonoran Desert or the unpredictable currents of the Rio Bravo. They hired a *coyote*, or migrant smuggler, who hatched a plan: the boys would be outfitted in dresses and use the birth certificates of a couple of girls around their age, then they could be driven across the border and returned to their parents on the other side. But, frightened and tearful, the boys refused to wear the dresses or board a vehicle without their parents. They ended up crossing on foot with Natalia through a hole in the fence, guided by a *coyote*. In California, they stayed with a cousin before flying to Florida.

The decision to leave their daughters behind was torturous for Natalia, but Lupe stood firm that this was for the best: besides the brutal work, their eldest, Maria, was just a couple of years away from earning her high school diploma and a certificate in accounting that could land her a comfortable job.

Decades later, Lalo wouldn't remember feeling apprehensive about beginning this new chapter. He was excited to make the trip, to see a different country, to get to know his father. Lalo and Jaime would be the third generation of their family to join the millions of Mexican migrants who traveled north to plow fields and pick produce in the United States, a country that had hungered for cheap labor since before its founding, but was ambivalent about the people who performed it.

José García Agueta, Lalo's maternal grandfather, came to the U.S. during World War II as part of the Bracero Program, an agreement between the United States and Mexico that addressed the wartime worker shortage by creating short-term labor contracts for Mexican men. In Lalo's home state of Guanajuato, potential workers traveled to the Irapuato recruiting center, then waited for weeks or months and endured humiliating tests, including being stripped naked and sprayed with DDT. They were promised housing, good working conditions, and insurance, but in practice a tiny fraction of employers honored those commitments. Guanajuato's central location was ideal for Bracero recruiters: far enough from the border for the flow of workers to be slowed or cut off at their discretion, but accessible by train when those who were selected made the journey north.

The workers sent life-sustaining money back home, but conditions were horrific from the start. Braceros were often worked beyond exhaustion, without regard for their welfare or even survival. Labor activist Henry Pope Anderson put it this way: "They are viewed as commodities, as objects, as chattels . . . you rent a bracero for six weeks or six months, and if he gets damaged, you don't care. You'll never see him again. You get next year's model—a newer, younger, healthier one." After the war, the Great Strike Wave of 1946 forced many industries to improve wages and regulate labor conditions, but the agricultural sector retained carte blanche: deportable at any moment, Bracero workers were unlikely to protest. What's more, the National Labor Relations Act of 1935, which guaranteed most workers the right to unionize, had excluded agricultural and domestic workers from the definition of "employee." At the time, a Congress dominated by white Southern Democrats had crafted the exclusion to prevent the economic empowerment of Black workers in the segregated South. Farmworkers had no federally protected right to unionize even during Lupe and Lalo's years in the fields, nor do they today.

When Natalia agreed to bring Lalo and Jaime north, she expected the work to be brutal and to lack basic comforts. She'd been raised in a farming family, and she held no illusions about the lifestyle. But it turned out the work in the U.S. was punishing not only physically, but psychologically.

Their new life on the road was taxing, grimy, poisonous. They moved from place to place following the crops. Each time they moved, Natalia tried to scrub down every surface, but the cockroaches slipped between the cracks in the kitchen cupboards, waiting for dark. The García family suffered the most in Florida. There, the attitude that labor performed by poor, brown people ought to be free had barely loosened its death grip. Citrus and tomatoes were king. The family was often sprayed with insecticide as they arrived at work, their skin made sticky with the chemicals. The pesticides left blisters on their hands, some of which never faded. Sometimes, as they drove through a checkpoint approaching a field, Lalo's parents would hide the boys under blankets to keep them from being sprayed. The lesson for young Lalo was clear: the health of the oranges was more important than his own.

Nothing prepared Lalo for the transition from one country to another. He likened it to the experience of a person who has never heard of an airplane, never seen so much as a drawing of one, suddenly boarding a 747 and lifting off into the sky. Everything, from his first sip of Yoo-hoo, to the smell of the refrigerated aisles at the 7–Eleven, to the vast landscapes of crops, hit his senses full-tilt.

Ten-year-old Lalo was a rambunctious kid, full of questions, fond of teasing, and a glutton for competition—his family members called him hyperactive, or just plain annoying. But he could also display a militaristic obedience when called upon. If the command was to gather oranges from the ground, all day long, or push needles from pine trees into piles so his father could fit them into a box and sell them for two dollars a bundle, he was dead set on being the fastest set of hands, and wouldn't complain if the task left him sticky with sap or punctured with splinters. Working as a team, the family would fill hundreds of boxes a day.

Sometimes, there was no work. They were between crops— cherries were ending, apples had not yet begun. Lupe taught his sons by example that you never stopped looking for work. Never. They'd find a church, offer to cut the grass. Sometimes they were rewarded with bags of rice and beans. Lupe was a machine, Lalo said. "I've never seen anyone work as hard as my father."

Born José Guadalupe García Guzmán in San José de las Pilas, Lupe was above average height among his Mexican peers, with broad shoulders and ropy muscles. His face was long, his eyes brown and pensive. Like the adult Lalo, his gaze conveyed conviction, a man who demanded respect, yet one who had a sense of humor and a buoyancy that defied his decades in the fields. His hair was full and dark, and he wore it parted on one side, swooping across his forehead. A thin mustache traced the edge of his upper lip. Over years of work, he grew accustomed to surviving on little sleep, working his body to its limit in service of his family's welfare. He was propelled by the call of his labor the way other men are compelled by God to rise and pray at dawn.

Lupe had spent most of his life without his own father. Ignacio García Guzmán had been murdered in the mid-1960s along with his brothers, ambushed after returning from work in the cornfields. This is a secondhand story now, and details are scarce; the sole relative who guards the tale is tight-lipped. What's known is that Ignacio was a powerful man in the village, who often settled disputes and might have had a number of enemies. The murder was an excruciating shock that came with eternal consequences for Lupe. After the ritual nine days of mourning, Lupe became the de facto caretaker for his family, with five younger siblings to feed and a farming operation to oversee. He was just a teenager, starting to think about striking out on his own, but now he had to raise his younger siblings first. At twenty-four, he started a flirtation with Natalia, who was still in her early teens. Their relationship was frowned upon by their families. Her parents offered to send her away to live with relatives in Sonora, to let her start over in a place where the courtship hadn't marred her reputation. But Lupe proposed marriage.

Natalia, born Salome García Acevedo, grew up in a small adobe house that neighbored Lupe's family home. Her father had a multi-purpose store, a small livestock operation, and a *paletería* that sold popsicles made of fresh fruit, but the income from these businesses was barely enough to provide for the couple's twelve children. On Three Kings Day, when Mexican children traditionally receive their Christmas gifts, Natalia remembers getting a doll fashioned from a piece of cardboard. She fussed over her new companion. When they were alone, she told her doll of her secret wish to go to school.

"I told my father, we have to go to school, but he said, 'For what? You're women, you don't need to study, you're going to marry.' So, we ran away, hiding from him, because we wanted to learn some-thing," Natalia said. "My childhood, when I think about it, it was very difficult because there wasn't time to play with dolls, to go out and play with my friends. It was all in the fields, in the house, because there wasn't a way to go and study. So, when we escaped, how were we going to learn to read and write? I learned a bit to write, but not totally to read. Because my father would come looking for me and if I wasn't at home, of course he's going to punish me. My mother said to my father, 'Just because they're girls doesn't mean they shouldn't study, they have to study.' In the end what happened with all of that? I wouldn't say that my life was bad with my father, no. But, at the first moment that I could leave, I looked for a way to leave. You look for another life."

Once they were married, Lupe was the one who went looking for that other life, for a way out of poverty, a virtual certainty in San José de las Pilas. He left Natalia in the village, pregnant.

"When I got married they said, 'Here are two plates, here are two cups, here is your pot to cook in and here is your kitchen. You know what you're going to do.'"

Natalia had spent most of her childhood helping her mother feed many mouths. They grew their food in the *milpa* system, which comes from the Nahuatl word *milli*, meaning cultivated field. There, corn, beans, and squash are intercropped to provide a mutually supportive ecosystem. Beans regenerate nitrogen in the soil, the corn stalk serves as a natural trellis for the tendrils of the beans to climb, and the wide leaves of the squash carpet the ground, keeping sunshine out, retaining moisture in the earth while preventing weeds. After the harvest, garbanzo beans were planted as a cover crop, fixing nitrogen into the soil. The method allows a family to be nourished from a small plot of land. Natalia and her family used everything the milpa supplied.

The squash—along with the plant's blossoms and vines—could be used as a filling for quesadillas. The garbanzos could be added to stock made from the drippings of pit-roasted sheep and eaten as a warming morning soup. The black beans could be cooked with onion and the herb epazote. But corn was the true basis of her family's diet. It could be eaten young, but most of the mature, dry corn was nixtamalized, a process of soaking the hard kernels in limewater—or water infused with calcium hydroxide—then washing and hulling them. The kernels were then ground to make *masa*, dough which could be fashioned into a variety of shapes. These included flat tortillas, *sopes*—small, thick circles, often topped with black beans—and *tlacoyos*, which are oblong and about twice as thick as a tortilla and are often stuffed with fava beans and topped with cheese and *nopales* (paddle-shaped cactus pads). Nixtamalization changes the chemical properties of corn and makes its nutrients bioavailable, a technique that has been used in the region for thousands of years.

By the time Natalia joined Lupe on the migrant path, she was twice as old as when they first began dating. Daily life without Lupe had become the norm. In his absence, she had run the household according to her judgment. Now, she deferred to Lupe, in a place she found maddening. She never had time to learn the rules or make a close friend, because within a month or two they were off to the next location.

Work was never hard to find—housing was the challenge. Sometimes they were waylaid in motels, blowing precious dollars on the room until they could find somewhere semi-permanent. Once in a while they'd come across a place that felt nominally welcoming, like a house in Florida on the edge of some woods, down a road paved white with seashells. There, Lalo felt free. But regardless of whether they were staying in a motel or a trailer with a dozen grown men, Lalo slept deeply. He was tired all the way to his bones.

Lupe rose at 4 a.m. to begin cooking, and gently woke Lalo and Jaime at 5 a.m. The early hours were blunted by two transcendent, intermingling smells: a hot stack of pancakes and a hot stack of flour tortillas, both made from scratch by Lupe while the rest of the family slept. In the absence of the corn masa they were accustomed to using to prepare tortillas in Mexico, they enjoyed larger flour tortillas, with fewer nutrients, but sublimely delicious when freshly made.

Lupe would combine flour, salt, and baking soda in the largest bowl he had, gently mix in the shortening with his fingertips, then add water and knead the sticky dough until it became silky to the touch. He'd roll the dough into balls the size of small limes and slap each piece in the palm of his hand to form a flat disc. Then, he'd lay these patties out on the counter or a baking sheet, cover them with a towel, and let them rest for fifteen minutes before using a rolling pin he'd fashioned out of a wooden broom handle to push them into thin circles. The last part, which he timed to coincide with the kids' wake-up call, was easy: he'd slide the rolled-out dough onto a hot pan until each tortilla puffed and was speckled with black char. They were just the right thickness: strong enough to hold whatever was folded inside and tender enough to yield easily when you took a bite.

Lupe used the fifteen-minute period when the dough was resting to prep the pancake batter. Once everyone had eaten a few pancakes, Natalia folded eggs, beans, and salsa into the tortillas to make tacos, which the kids ate in the pickup truck, sipping from cartons of chocolate milk. After their bellies were full, they'd lie down on a mattress Lupe had procured for the bed of the truck, a way to buy his sons a little more sleep. It could take them thirty minutes or two hours to get to the field.

How to describe a childhood that was at once so adult, so rootless, so laborious, and yet, in broad strokes and tiny moments, so happy? That's how an adult Lalo describes these times: when his father climbed the branches of a tree and shook them with his whole body, coercing the citrus to the ground so he and Jaime and Natalia might gather the fruit into a massive tub that would cumulatively earn them nine dollars. When he collected a chip for each bucket of tomatoes picked. When they ate a homemade breakfast together. When he put on a headlamp and peeked into the mushroom beds in Chester, Pennsylvania, for the first time. When his father studied the road atlas and decided to take the scenic route from one state to another. Happy.

Lalo had been scolded for years about his *travesuras*, or mischief. He never could sit still. In the fields, he was able to channel this energy to incredible results. Instead of pushing the limits by breaking his parents' rules, he pushed them by exceeding what anyone might expect a ten-year-old to pick in a day. His brother Jaime looked on askance: "If Lalo had the choice to work or play, he would rather work." Jaime didn't love the work; he didn't hate it either. He just wanted normalcy. A home, a few friends, maybe even a spot on a sports team.

In the Wauchula, Florida, citrus groves or the Belding, Michigan, apple orchards, Lalo quickly understood the scoring system: if you earned the most, you were the best. Still in elementary school, he set his sights on twenty-year-olds in their physical prime, determined to outpick them. Often, he'd succeed. Not all crops were equal. Lalo liked the fast work best: you could shake oranges from the tree. Strawberries were slow. You had to pick them and select the pretty ones to place on top, packaging them for the supermarket right in the field.

Though he and Jaime were still children, their presence in the fields didn't raise any eyebrows. Lalo routinely saw preschoolers filling buckets, babies wrapped in *rebozos* tied to their mothers' backs. The country's child labor laws were more relaxed when it came to agricultural work, but even so, most everything that Lalo and Jaime did was illegal. Theoretically, children as young as ten can pick fruits and vegetables, but they have to be given special permission that is virtually never granted due to concerns about pesticide exposure. And yet, because there was nowhere else to leave young kids when school was out of session, especially during the summer harvest, the sight of children working in the fields was common. Farmworkers are often paid per piece or per pound during the harvest, and it was easy enough for employers to look the other way as children tossed fruit into the family bucket. Beyond the economic imperative, there wasn't much else to do in the fields besides help. As soon as an investigator came on the scene, the children could be hustled out of sight or could pretend they weren't working.

A couple of decades before Lalo worked in the fields, Truman E. Moore dramatized a cat-and-mouse game between inspectors and kids in his book *The Slaves We Rent*. A worker puts down his hamper and, looking out at a clear blue sky, tells the man next to him that "it sure looks like rain." The message goes up and down the rows, as children drop their boxes. "The children hid beyond the road in a small clearing in a clump of scrub oaks. From here they could see the man leave. It was their favorite game. Hiding from the inspector was about the only thing that broke up the long hours in the field. In the camp they played hide and seek this way. When you were 'it' you were the inspector. But it was more fun when there was a real inspector."

When there were rumblings of an inspection afoot in a typical vegetable field, Lalo and Jaime would wait in the pickup truck and listen to the radio until they were given the all-clear. In orchards and citrus groves, they might try their luck at hiding.

Lalo helped his family earn $200 to $300 a day, filling bucket after bucket of onions, cucumbers, oranges, apples, limes. Had there been a scoreboard, Lalo's name would have been at the top, right under Lupe's. But away from the fields, at the schools up and down their route, Lalo was failing. He didn't speak the language, and he never stayed anywhere long enough to find a teacher who might champion his education. There were a handful of migrant advocates sprinkled through the public school system, but barriers were enormous: parents who didn't speak English, kids who arrived in November and left in April, poverty demanding that they work in the fields instead of spending time doing homework, sleeping or, at times, attending class.

When Lalo did make it to the ever-unfamiliar classrooms, he retreated inward. He didn't know how to make friends, an unfortunate problem for a boy who had to start all over several times a year. He'd seek out the other immigrant kids, who sometimes hailed from India or China. On the inside, he was hungry for knowledge. But, short on English and continuity, he scored low on every assessment.

He and Jaime were bullied in the schoolyards of southern Georgia. At recess, a bunch of kids approached them: Hey, I have an onion field that needs picking! How much would that cost me? That memory would resurface in Lalo's head for decades, unsolicited. In the cafeteria line, a girl stopped Lalo. Hey Eduardo, she said, you wore that same pair of pants yesterday! "I said 'No, no,' in my broken English, but of course I understood her." The girl was adamant. Yes, she said, you wore that same pair of pants yesterday. "Obviously, I wore the same pair of pants all fucking week. I only had two pairs." In the classroom, teachers would sit Lalo down, along with a few other kids, and wheel in the television cart, perhaps with some half-hearted hope that Harrison Ford would teach them English as he tried to escape the Temple of Doom. Some teachers left a positive impression, but Jaime had a stronger recollection of the wood paddle in a Florida school, the racist nicknames one Georgia teacher assigned to all her students of color. Lupe and Natalia never called much attention to the strange new racial dynamics in this strange new country. Lalo perceived the tension as a change in the atmosphere that seemed to thicken the further south they traveled. They were simultaneously welcomed—there were jobs to do, after all—and resented.

Racism and farmwork were, of course, intertwined before the nation's founding, when the labor of enslaved Africans artificially drove down the price of food and cash crops. In the mid-nineteenth century, Chinese immigrants fleeing war and famine came to California in pursuit of the Gold Rush. Many would become agricultural laborers before the Chinese Exclusion Act—enacted in part to protect the wages of white workers—largely banned their entry. At that time, African Americans and Native Americans could be legally charged with vagrancy, arrested, and forced to work, often to death. Then came the eugenics movement, at the time referred to as a "science," which asserted a racial hierarchy among mankind and advocated for a human hand in selecting genetically superior offspring. At the height of eugenicist fever in the United States, the 1924 Johnson–Reed Act enshrined this ranking system into law, setting immigration quotas based on the perceived desirability of the addition of different nationalities to the U.S. gene pool. Still, there were fields to plow and crops to pick; partly due to the pressure to fill these difficult, low-paying jobs, the law set no quota for those hailing from countries in the Americas. While skepticism of eugenics would grow as news of the Third Reich's cruel policies toward the disabled made its way to the United States and scientific research debunked its tropes, its warped logic would remain embedded in the DNA of the U.S. immigration system.

In 1960, on the day after Thanksgiving, CBS broadcast an exposé titled *Harvest of Shame* about the horrific conditions of migrant workers. The opening shows workers being recruited in Florida as Edward R. Murrow narrates: "this is the way the humans who harvest the food for the best-fed people in the world get hired. One farmer looked at this and said, 'We used to own our slaves; now we just rent them.'" The politicians who terminated the Bracero Program in 1964 hoped U.S.-born fieldworkers, no longer in competition with foreign labor, would be offered better wages. Instead, farmers changed crops, automated jobs, or reduced production. The Labor Department's desperate attempts to harvest crops in the face of the new labor shortage included recruiting high school athletes; as it turned out, they couldn't hack it.

Lupe began migrating to the U.S. just after the Bracero Program ended. He couldn't swim, but he managed to cross the Rio Bravo; in Tijuana he folded himself into the trunk of a car. In California, where he picked almonds and strawberries, Mexican and Filipino farmworkers came together to protest their low wages and dangerous working conditions, though one of the movement's leaders, Cesar Chavez, was initially unwelcoming to foreign-born migrants. In 1975, the United Farm Workers won a landmark victory that enshrined their right to organize in California law, though they still had no such federal protection. Other states were slow to follow suit and today less than 1 percent of farmworkers belong to a union.

Workers like Lupe who surreptitiously traversed the border in the 1970s and 1980s found that it wasn't difficult to make it across undetected. Even if you were caught, such entries were rarely prosecuted. The H–2A guest worker program filled the gap left behind by the Bracero Program, but its features made it similarly fertile for exploitation, locking workers into specific jobs and relying on recruiters who were quick to blacklist any worker who complained. Those who chose to bypass officialdom found that neither government was particularly eager to stop them: there was still a demand for labor north of the border, and for the lifeline of remittances sent to the south.

Ronald Reagan's mixed immigration record is best remembered for the massive amnesty of 1986, which paired increased border enforcement with a path to citizenship. Undocumented immigrants who met certain conditions and had entered the country before 1982 could wait for eighteen months, then make a payment of $185 and receive their green cards, provided they learned minimal English, demonstrated some knowledge of the history and government of the United States, and showed "good moral character." Lupe enrolled in the second phase, which offered the same opportunity to agricultural workers. Some of the 2.7 million new permanent residents were eager to become U.S. citizens; others, like Lupe and Natalia, were more interested in steady work, since high unemployment in Mexico made it tough to go home. Having papers gave them more options— the possibility of going into professions beyond agriculture, of moving to different regions of the United States. As Mexican residents made these connections, they were able to help relatives find work, and back in states like Guanajuato the hopes and plans of their families began to shift.

"Remittances feed the imaginations of the young," said Jorge Durand, an anthropologist who researches Mexican migration. "They say, 'I'm going to leave, I want to earn dollars. I want to build a new house, or buy a truck. I want a different lifestyle.' They go thinking they'll be able to earn enough in two or three years to build that house, and at the end of that period they don't have enough to build anything."

Indeed, Lupe kept returning to the U.S. year after year in an attempt to earn a life-changing amount, but it wasn't until Natalia, Lalo, and Jaime crossed the border to join him that they could finally make enough to begin saving a little. As that money was socked away, they began to imagine what it might be like to build a life north of the border. When a profitable crop was being harvested, Lalo and Jaime gave up going to school altogether. "I can remember my dad saying, 'If you're really smart, and you really want to go to school, you can catch up, you can catch on,'" Jaime said. "But that wasn't really the case, because we couldn't get adjusted."

Natalia watched her sons struggle, but she had barely attended school herself and at parent–teacher conferences she couldn't communicate. Meanwhile, her daughters, Maria and Isela, were living alone in the house in the Estado de México, with an aunt and uncle who lived on the next block as supervision. Natalia felt as if she'd been cleaved in two; the half of her that roamed the U.S. was perpetually on edge, the half that remained psychically in Mexico was impotent. There were no cell phones to send a text, no video chats to see her daughters' faces. Natalia made quick work of finding the payphone closest to each new residence, then traded her bills for a tall stack of quarters for a five-minute reunion. The girls needed school, and they needed a different childhood than she'd had, Natalia told herself. It was safer for them to stay in Mexico.

Out of all of their stops, Natalia hated Florida with a special passion. After a life spent in the mountains of central Mexico, the Florida heat was like an invisible bully, pushing her further over the edge day by day. By the time they arrived at the citrus grove in the morning, their clothes were already soaked through and her thick hair sponged in the humidity, frustrating her attempts to style it. Natalia took on the Sisyphean task of keeping them all clean and dry. She'd bring three changes of clothes a day, even if cycling through them only bought brief moments free of the mix of pesticides, condensation, and sweat.

She'd wake from a dream and run out of the trailer, gasping for a rejuvenating breath of fresh air, only to be met by the thick and stagnant night. Often in those dark hours, she'd insist that Lalo accompany her to the hospital to find out what was wrong. In Lalo's basic

English, he'd try to convey the pain his mother felt in feminine places, the functions of which he didn't yet comprehend. Lalo stared at the doctor, who didn't seem to understand what his mother was trying to communicate. He felt like he was buried underground. Take two Tylenol, rest—usually, that was the most advice she got. "Now that I think about it," Lalo said, "they were trying to say, 'All this drama you have going on in your life, not having your daughters, having to see your kids work like adults, living in a country where you don't belong and working in the conditions you're working in, that's what's causing all of your problems.' You know?"

Decades later, the family still didn't know what Natalia should have been diagnosed with, only that her suffering was very real. "I never adapted, I was living my worst nightmare. I never felt well. I got depressed by the changes in climate, altitude. I think it was also being so far from my daughters. I couldn't sleep, I felt so depressed. I couldn't explain what was happening to me."

Lalo watched Natalia's transformation from the enforcer, the nurturer, the rock, to a harried, disoriented woman whose dutiful work feeding and clothing them masked her fragility. He didn't know what to do for her. He just knew she was suffering all the time, and he couldn't make the suffering go away.

As Natalia ached, the girls suffered, too, missing their mother. Maria, who had the photo-ready beauty of a soap opera star and a fierce, understated confidence, was working toward a degree in accounting. Isela, an introvert with dark, straight hair and large, searching eyes, retreated further into herself when Natalia left. Lupe rarely saw the girls, but Natalia went to Mexico to see them two or three times a year. Even before he departed with her mother and brothers, Maria had been angry with her father for spending most of his time so far away. On the phone, she'd beg him to come back. When he visited, she waged her campaign more forcefully. They'd both end up in tears.

Maria was curious about her family's life north of the border. The picture her parents painted had little in common with the images exported globally by Hollywood. They were at the bottom of the heap; their days were *puro trabajo*. Lupe liked to take liberties with the road atlas, chancing a few stops to cool the engine as they took the scenic route, but his detours were always through the nation's rural landscapes, never to sightsee. In all those years, they never met Mickey Mouse at Disney World or veered off course to see the Lincoln Memorial or the New York City skyline, or even to take a walk along the Florida beach. Lupe made time for just one activity: on Sundays, if clergy didn't make a visit to the fields, they'd find a church, often little more than a room in a family home with a makeshift pulpit and a cross on the wall. They'd sit and wait for the local priest to drive from his first service of the day in a bigger town nearby. After they prayed, they went back to work.

Each year, as they earned more, the anxiety that had initially manifested as an eerie vibration began to thrum insistently beneath the surface of Natalia's skin. It was present even during times of success, and robbed her of the contentment that ought to arrive when, having pulled yourself up the rungs of a ladder, you can enjoy a brief rest and take in the view. "I thought, 'This can't be my life! This can't be a life for my children!' You'd make a pair of friends in one state, and six weeks later you wouldn't have them anymore. That's how it was, never stable. How could you ever feel that someone's your friend? They're not. Lupe always said, 'Be your own friend, because real friends? We don't have those. In the important moments, you don't have a friend with you.'"

They were saving money, this Natalia knew. But where had it gotten them? When would it be enough? At least in the Estado de México, the house had made visible what Lupe's years of work had accomplished. Now, itinerant, they moved from one semblance of a home to the next, on a journey that switched directions and doubled back, until the word "destination" had lost all meaning.

CHAPTER TWO

ESCOFFIER REINCARNATE

LALO'S TWELFTH YEAR marked a sea change for his family: his sisters Maria and Isela finally crossed the border for their first-ever chance to live as a unified family in the United States. Maria, the oldest, was filled with expectation. But when they arrived at the trailer in Okeechobee where the family was finishing the citrus season, she was sickened. Florida was always the toughest part of the route, and when they drove up to the trailer, Lupe seemed to suddenly take stock of his surroundings through his daughters' eyes. They couldn't possibly stay here! They began the drive to Ohio, to follow Roma tomatoes and pickling cucumbers, the next day.

Maria had by then graduated from high school with a certificate in accounting that could have been parlayed into an office job. Lupe couldn't understand why she was wasting the credential and the years of education it required by coming to the United States. But the subject that called to Maria most, the one she was desperate to understand, was her father, a man who had been physically absent from so much of her childhood. What was this place that had taken him, that had then taken her mother and brothers and had left her and Isela alone in the house in the Estado de México for more than two years? Unless she made the journey, Maria realized, she'd never get to know Lupe. The only way was to stand alongside him, to perform the labor he had dedicated decades to and register its toll. After a couple of weeks she could barely sit on the toilet as her exhausted muscles seized in protest. Seeing her father's trade close-up was mystifying. "How was it possible for him to endure so much? So, so, so, so much?"

After Ohio, where tiny cucumber thorns chafed against their skin, there was some respite in Michigan, with stone fruit, blueberries, apples, then fall colors. Perhaps the girls would get to see a snow-fall before heading south. When the Garcías arrived in Michigan that year, the children were turned away by a farmer. Lalo, Jaime, and Isela walked home while Maria, Natalia, and Lupe spent the day working at the orchard. When they returned, they encountered a banquet of peaches blushing shades of sunset red and yellow, cherries and plums gleaming darkly: the spoils that the children had gathered on their walk.

Each year they traveled to Vidalia, Georgia, where they lived in a trailer down a coffee-colored road, close to a convenience store that sold bags of boiled peanuts, the aisles lined with watermelons. That crop brought its own wildness even to the industrial fields—the vines took over the landscape with their unruly pattern. In Vidalia, they spent weeks hovered in a squatting position above the sandy soil, digging out the town's namesake onions. Some days they swept pine needles from under the trees to box and sell as mulch.

It was in Georgia that a twelve-year-old Lalo walked into the piney woods with his father's rifle and heard a crinkling of leaves underfoot. A deer stepped into the clearing and Lalo pointed the gun and pulled the trigger. Nothing happened. Panicking, he hit the safety, tried again. Nothing. Again, he hit the safety as the first deer pranced out of sight and a second came into view. Lalo shot and hit the animal, watching its graceful legs crumple and its body pitch to the ground. It was a young male deer, with a puffy white tail like a boll of cotton. He staggered home with the animal draped over his shoulders and Natalia cooked the meat in a *guisado*, or stew, with *salsa de chile pasilla*. The meat was tough and lean, but the memory of young Lalo with the deer over his shoulders and a smile on his face stuck with the family forever.

These were the moments the sisters had hoped to see when they came north, the shared experiences that would become treasured memories, then family legends. But they were few and far between. In the fields, they came to share the vision of the U.S. that the family had recounted by phone: a place of grim work, loneliness, and exploitation. And yet, the daily competition to outearn his fellow workers seemed to motivate Lalo. In a field with a hundred rows and sixty workers, Lalo would start the shift by running from row to row, planting a few seeds in each one, so his family could claim the lion's share of the work. Maria, a city girl, watched with horror as her brother created as much work for them as possible. She felt overwhelmed and out of place. "People would look at my mother and say, 'Why are you bringing your daughters here? They have such pretty skin, they're not like us. Why are you bringing them out here under the sun?' "

Before the girls' arrival, the family had moved along the migrant route led by Lupe, whose decades of experience had rendered the difficult journey routine. But with fresh eyes, Maria, shocked by the unsafe and unfair conditions, began to protest, throwing the family's future into question. She departed to live with Natalia's sister in Atlanta, and got a job at McDonald's. But over the next year, she con-

tinued to think about the rest of the family in the fields and the poi-
sons they were exposed to every day, the pittance they were paid. Her
outrage grew. They should all get off the road! There was steady work
to be had in Atlanta. Maybe Jaime and Lalo stood a chance of graduating from high school. Lupe resisted at first, but during their final
months working in Florida, Natalia had her worst run-in with the
medical establishment. A doctor performed a routine pap smear and
returned a diagnosis of cancer. Natalia, already struggling to fend off
depression and anxiety, went into shock. Witnessing her suffering, an
acquaintance of the family's from the fields made Lupe an extraordinary offer: he had a thousand dollars saved up and urged Lupe to
take it. You need to send your wife to Mexico, he said, because she's
going to die here.

They accepted. With the money, Natalia returned to Mexico
alone in the midst of a breakdown of body and mind. There, doctors performed more tests, determined that she was cancer-free, and
urged her to return to Florida to demand answers from the hospital.
It turned out they'd given Natalia the results from another patient.
In the meantime, she'd suffered a nervous breakdown. "That was the
root of the depression that poisoned me," Natalia said. Lupe finally
conceded that perhaps Maria was right, they should get off the road
once and for all. They decided to join Maria and their other relatives,
and give the northern Atlanta suburb of Chamblee a try.

It should have been a time of peace and happiness for Natalia:
she was settled, she had her whole family under one roof for the first
time since she was a child. But she was changed, on a host of medi-
cations to ease her nerves and allow her to sleep. From then on, she
seemed to be moving through a fog that wavered in density. For
Lalo, the mother of his early childhood never returned. The woman
who remained with them was indomitable, yes, in the sense that she

continued working and caring for the family with vigor and without complaint. But she remained at a remove, a distance that could be detected in her eyes, in her faded memories, in a hesitancy that Lalo had never noted before.

In Georgia, Lalo and his family set about putting down roots. In doing so, they joined a growing experiment among Mexican immigrants in the U.S. South: seeing the opportunities afforded by an economic boom, they were moving to areas that had previously been insulated from Mexican migration, as Jim Crow laws and the racist legacy that persisted had deterred potential newcomers while creating high levels of poverty and an abundance of low-wage labor. Radical changes began in the 1980s, when plentiful jobs, changing immigration policy, and inexpensive housing drew immigrants to the area. Georgia quadrupled its Latino population during the 1990s, a change that was especially evident in their chosen destination of Chamblee. There, between 1980 and 2000, the population shifted from 89 percent white to 54 percent Latino, 14.5 percent Asian and 5 percent Black. New arrivals were drawn by the two local subway stops and the number of low-cost rental units.

None of the places where the Garcías lived in the U.S. had been idyllic, but Chamblee had its own set of problems.

"There were people drinking, lots of police, gunshots and that sort of thing," Lalo said. "People were super racist, and I remember most of the young guys who lived in those apartment buildings were people who I later associated with—gang members." Lupe doubled down on his rules. No saggy pants, no rap music at home.

The change from countryside to suburb was most radical for Lupe. For decades, he had been bound to the seasons, working and living in conditions that were dangerous, lonely, and precarious. But he'd also spent his entire life working outdoors; convincing him to leave that way of life behind was a battle. It confounded Maria that he could have been so loyal to a line of work that regarded him with no allegiance and paid him almost nothing. How, she wondered, could he put up with it? Later, she'd reason that he probably liked the work because he seemed like a happy person, always ready with a joke, always with joy in his heart. In this newly rooted life, he found himself hunched over the sink in the bleak kitchen of a Jalisco-style restaurant called El Torero in a Roswell, Georgia, strip mall. Every bone in his body ached to be outdoors.

A few months after they moved to Chamblee, a family they'd worked beside in Vidalia invited them to a picnic spot along a river. They were warned by fellow picnickers not to wade out beyond the shallows, but the water looked calm, the undertow and tree roots invisible from the surface. Jaime and Lalo were splashing around, then Lalo suddenly seemed to get deeper. Natalia watched his hand go up. At first she thought he was playing, until she realized he wasn't. No one in the family knew how to swim. Lupe hustled into the water in his heavy boots and jeans. Natalia stood screaming on the riverbank as she watched Lupe lurch for a handful of Lalo's shirt, hoisting him to the surface before a passing boat pulled them out.

Lalo was always pushing the limits. It was clear to his parents that boredom was the enemy. That summer, Lupe sent Lalo away to Louisville, Kentucky, to work with his uncle at a Mexican restaurant, bringing chips and water to the tables. When he returned, Lalo's cousin told him about a job at the Georgia Grille, a casual Southwest-style dinner spot named for Georgia O'Keeffe and known for its lobster enchiladas. For six months he washed dishes, content with the paycheck. But, ever the enemy of idleness, Lalo picked up prep work when there weren't enough dishes to clean.

Scott Adair, a thirty-five-year-old, cooked alongside him. Lalo was fifteen, and most people assumed he was little more than a good worker with a limited grasp of English. But Adair noticed the way Lalo cut tomatoes for *pico de gallo*: in a perfect brunoise—one-eighth-inch cubes. He'd go through an entire box of tomatoes in less than thirty minutes, and his technique never seemed to suffer for the speed. Adair gringocized his given name, Eduardo, to dub him "Fast Eddie," as he climbed the ladder from dishwasher to prep to salads, and then the line.

Lalo's knowledge of cooking came primarily from Natalia. She didn't have impressive knife skills—she hacked vegetables apart in uneven chunks—but what she lacked in formal training, she more than made up for with her palate, her impeccable sense of balance. She intuited the exact amount of onion that should go in her beans, the way the acid from a lime brightened a dish, the importance of the herbaceous note of epazote or cilantro to finish, just how much to add, and whether it should be cooked or raw. Natalia would riff on the Mexican classics—she called these variations her "little experiments." She wasn't using liquid nitrogen to freeze drops of vanilla, she wasn't making a bean foam or a mint-flavored oil, or even using a cookbook. What she did was add a small twist, one that a non-Mexican audience might not realize was a twist at all. She'd add a vegetable not normally found in a guisado, but one that seemed to enhance the flavors. She found originality in her kitchen, and wasn't afraid to deviate from an accepted norm. Sometimes this arose from a sense of adventure, but more often her inventiveness was mothered by necessity; like so many of her counterparts, cooking in small towns in the South and Midwest, she'd scour the grocery shelves and try to recreate a taste of home with a long list of substitutions.

Instead of tomatillos, the tart green cousins of tomatoes that grow inside a sticky, paper-like husk, Natalia tried to summon their

tang from unripe tomatoes. Cilantro she'd buy fresh in large quantities, then she'd dehydrate the leaves and save them for later. A few
farmers in Ohio, seeing a demand among their workers, planted
chiles, but mostly she relied on a dried stash she'd purchase at small
Mexican bodegas when they were in Florida. When she cooked, she
reconstituted them in water. Daily salsas lacked the fresh, acidic zing
of the serranos she was accustomed to; often, they lacked any heat.

Natalia's experiments were, in essence, another contribution to
a lineage of culinary invention that adapted the ingredients of a foreign culture in the face of adversity.

———

One of the first points of cultural encounter between conquistador Hernán Cortes and the native peoples of the landmass known
today as Mexico was food, offered by emissaries of Aztec *tlatoani*,
or emperor, Moctezuma II to the Spanish naval crew that landed
in Veracruz in 1519. They were given "very well-made tamales, sent
still hot, ordinary tortillas and tamales with beans, round like thick
rods, and all sorts of cooked and grilled fowl, quail, barbecued deer,
rabbits, ground chile, many kinds of cooked quelites or greens, and
fruits like plantains, custard apples, guavas and chayote squash,"
according to indigenous chronicler Hernando Alvarado Tezozómoc,
a descendent of Moctezuma. This first offering conveys the bounty
of native ingredients that were unknown to the foreigners—corn
and chiles among them—and the vast differences in preparation,
including the virtual absence of cooking fat. The offering seems like
a friendly gesture of welcome, but historian Sarah Bak-Geller Corona
writes that the exchange is more complex than meets the eye, betray-
ing "the thoroughly political character of actors," both Spanish and
Aztec: Moctezuma ordered his messengers to assess the foreigners'

response to the food, so that he might be able to determine if the new arrivals were gods or impostors. The Spanish, on the other hand, suspicious of being poisoned, told the Aztec messengers to taste the food first. Then, after the Spanish ate this bounteous meal, they gave the messengers some stale bread in return, along with wine. This set the stage for unequal exchanges to come: indigenous groups supplied gold, silver, embroidery, and jewels, while the Spanish celebrated opportunities to trick them into accepting cheap ribbons and sewing needles.

The bread sent back to Tenochtitlan was analyzed with care. Priests determined that these offerings were "like human food: big, white, not heavy, as if made of straw. Like corn cane fiber, and tasting of corn cane marrow. A bit sweet, a bit syrupy: they are eaten like honey, they are sweet food."

Between 1519 and 1526, Cortés sent back five letters to King Ferdinand and Queen Isabella. Food is mentioned often, usually in the context of an overall impression of plenty in these impressive cities, at least one of which was "more beautiful to look at than any in Spain." At one market, he estimated that 60,000 people came daily to shop and sell their goods, including precious metals, wood, brick, and tiles, as well as charcoal, ceramics, shells, and feathers. There were streets with an astounding diversity of birds for sale (among them, wild ducks, turtledoves, parrots, and eagles), apothecaries that sold liquid ointments, barber shops, and still other sections where vendors offered "every sort of vegetable, especially onions, leeks, garlic, common cress and watercress, borage, sorrel, teasels and artichokes." He encountered maguey syrup, "much better than most syrups," salted fish and maize, "both as grain and as bread." Cortés admitted he couldn't provide a complete list; the items for sale were too varied, and in many cases, he simply didn't know what they were called. "Lastly there is amongst them every consequence of good order and courtesy," with land that is well used, "leaving no place untilled."

These references are far overshadowed by his self-mythologizing descriptions of mass homicide perpetrated in the name of Christ and country. After this initial encounter, Cortés began a journey west with his men. He had no idea how many people lived in the region—Tenochtitlan was among the most populous cities in the world at the time of the conquest—nor could he fathom the nature of the conflicts between the area's distinct groups. Cortés haunted the Valley of Mexico with death, but his men did not bring Tenochtitlan down on their own. Rather, just 1 to 2 percent of those at battle were Spanish. The majority were members of other city-states and, in many cases, their alliances and conflicts predated the arrival of Cortés. Smallpox was also a major factor. As it was eradicated in 1980, we are blessedly ignorant of its symptoms; but, at the time, hundreds of thousands of inhabitants found themselves suddenly covered with sores that grew into pustules the size of peas, scabbed, and fell off. Many died, and others were left permanently scarred and even blind.

The overwhelming majority of colonizers who arrived in New Spain were men. Rape, intermarriage, and concubinage led to the emergence of a mixed-race population, and European authorities, intent on maintaining their primacy, began to craft an increasingly detailed caste system. Casta paintings, which typically had sixteen panels, diagrammed the terminology that was used to categorize children born to different combinations of parents. In most of these paintings, the first panel portrayed a Spanish father, an indigenous mother, and their child—a mestizo; the term mestizaje would come to signify the blending of native and foreign cultures, including in the region's cuisine. Since few women arrived from Spain before

the mid-sixteenth century, virtually all food was prepared by indigenous women using established methods. That's not to say Spaniards
didn't long for their Mediterranean diet—wine, almonds, and olive
oil were imported—but these ingredients became luxuries rather
than customs of daily life. They adapted to pre-Hispanic foodways,
which have endured to modern times. Tamales and *atole*,* a breakfast based on indigenous foods (beans, chiles, tomatoes, cacao) and
preparations, is still one of the most common meals for workers buying something quickly on the street in the morning. Mexican food is
often discussed as a marriage of flavors from Europe and the Americas, and while it's true that the ingredients of both continents indeed
merged (the almonds in *mole*† that keep company with chiles and
chocolate, the *pambazo* bread that gets dunked in guajillo chile salsa
and fried), most of the culinary concepts we identify today as "Mexican" pre-date the conquest. Many of the items on the list of foods
sent by Moctezuma can be found on contemporary Mexican tables,
along with salsa, atole, tlacoyos, *pulque*,‡ and hot chocolate—though
today's version of the drink has plenty of added sugar. The introduction of pork was the most significant alteration to pre-Hispanic

---

* *Atole* (pronounced ah-TOH-lay) is a pre-Hispanic hot beverage made with corn
masa and usually sweetened and flavored with ingredients like cinnamon, chocolate,
vanilla, or fruit.

† *Mole* (pronounced MOH-lay) may be related to either or both of two words: *molli*,
Nahuatl for sauce, and *moler*, Spanish for grind. Either term is descriptive of this wide
variety of thick sauces, usually involving many finely ground ingredients including
chiles, nuts, herbs, spices, vegetables and, sometimes, chocolate. Today, mole is prepared
with both native ingredients and ingredients that were brought to the Americas from
Europe. Moles range in color from moss green to crimson to black-brown, and may be
served with fish, turkey, as a tamale filling, with rice, enchiladas . . . the list goes on.

‡ Pulque is a fermented pre-Hispanic drink made from the sap of the maguey plant,
with a viscous texture, often flavored with fruit. Pulque has about the same alcohol
content as beer.

cooking, which had previously utilized little to no fat. Lard changed the way many dishes could be prepared. Across the region, the corn masa in tamales became supple with lard. In Michoacan, pork was sizzled in its own fat for carnitas. In the Yucatán, red achiote seeds harvested from the bristled pods of the annatto tree were ground into a paste and used to marinate pork before the meat was wrapped in banana leaves and barbecued in the ground—the iconic *cochinita pibil.** Ingredients from the Americas found their way overseas as well. Corn, tomatoes, chiles, and cacao have inextricably linked themselves with how we imagine food, from East to West: they made possible kimchi in Korea, rogan josh in India, jollof rice across West Africa, chocolate truffles in France, and pizza in Italy.

———

Lalo watched his mother cook carnitas, chilaquiles, and tamales in their improvised kitchens. He worshipped the flavors of her table. But he never imagined that he would one day be a chef. Lalo hadn't decided to work in restaurants because he heard a calling from on high; a cousin working at the Georgia Grille gave word that there was a job opening, and since his family had decided to settle down at last, he needed something local to keep him busy and keep the money rolling in. He devoured the school lunches during the years that his family spent in rural Georgia, where fried chicken, collard greens, and macaroni and cheese were doled out onto his tray. But his fascination with food didn't seem all that special; his whole fam-

———

* Predating the Spanish conquest, Mayan cooks prepared slow-roasted meat in an underground pit, or *pib*, lined with leaves and stones. *Cochinita pibil*, the iteration most commonly eaten today, was developed after pork was introduced to the continent. The pork emerges from the pit tender and juicy, with a deep red hue, and is typically served with corn tortillas, habanero salsa, and pickled onions, a bright contrast to the rich, fatty meat.

ily enjoyed cooking and eating. Didn't everyone love food? The Garcías had relatives who worked in kitchens, and Lalo knew from his
father's time at El Torero that kitchen work was grueling: washing
a never-ending stack of dishes, bussing the picked-over plates from
grungy tables. Kitchen jobs were not the jobs you dreamed about.

Unlike Lalo, his fellow cook Scott Adair had arrived in the
kitchen with a dream in his heart. In 1989, he'd left a stable career
in marketing at his family's company to become a chef. One year
earlier, *Food and Wine* magazine had released its first ever list of
Best New Chefs, heralding a growing obsession with food culture
in the United States. The names on that list? Daniel Boulud, Hubert
Keller, Thomas Keller, Gordon Hamersley, Gordon Naccarato, Robert McGrath, Bruce Auden, Frank Brigtsen, Johanne Killeen and
George Germon, and Rick Bayless. It's no wonder Adair could imagine himself joining the lineup: the magazine had almost exclusively
selected a group of white men to applaud.

Adair couldn't afford to stage, or apprentice, for the chefs he
admired. He needed a paycheck. His family wasn't especially pleased
to see their son follow his dream. When they heard the word "chef,"
that rarified group of food celebrities was not what came to mind.
Adair first went to culinary school and then looked for work. His in-
laws were friends with Georgia Grille chef and owner Karen Hilliard,
and, much to the relief of his parents and his wife, he landed a job.

In the early 1990s, Atlanta's dining scene was starting to bloom.
The announcement of the 1996 Summer Olympics brought with it
an avalanche of investment, including tony office towers with space
for restaurants on the lobby floor. Most of the city's restaurant culture was casual, dominated by diners, soul food restaurants, and
tearooms, along with the banh mi, lo mein, and enchiladas in new
immigrant communities near Lalo's apartment. Atlanta was also

home to Coca-Cola's headquarters, and the drink's red and white logo was ubiquitous.

Atlanta native Karen Hilliard opened the Georgia Grille in 1990 as an industrious self-taught cook. When Lalo came to work for her a few years later, she was struck by his work ethic and his sheer speed. She watched as he prepped vegetables, blasting through stacks of tomatoes and carrots, competing against an oblivious kitchen of cooks. He tore up his fingers time and again, and Hilliard drove him to the hospital for stitches. When he returned, he'd put a glove on his hand and go back to work.

Farmwork had required Lalo to mimic and quickly master new skills—whether you were boxing pine straw or picking cherries, you had to develop a technique and then sustain it for hours, days, weeks. In the fields, Lupe's instructions were brief. Lalo learned by watching, then took off at a sprint. In the kitchen, Lalo studied Adair as he executed techniques he'd paid tens of thousands of dollars to learn in culinary school. Within days, Lalo would be performing them better and faster. Soon he began to make food for Adair to taste, showcasing his discerning palate, inherited from Natalia. It was like watching a preternaturally talented young athlete practice: in Lalo, Adair saw the combined qualities of aptitude, work ethic, and physical ability harmonize. And whereas a great tennis player might have the ideal combination of strength and agility to rule the court, or a basketball player the height to give her an edge as she springs toward the hoop, Adair admired Lalo's hands: "They're like claws! They're God's gift to him." Those hands told Adair he would never supersede this cocky kid, no matter how long or hard he worked.

When Adair left the Georgia Grille to start his own catering business, he asked Lalo to join him. He would pick Lalo up at 4:30 a.m. and the two would prepare a catered breakfast for a local bank.

He'd drop Lalo at high school, pick him up at 3:30 p.m. to prep again, and then send him off to the Georgia Grille.

Soon, Adair opened his first restaurant, a small Southwestern spot called the Purple Cactus Cafe. When Adair arrived at work, Lalo would be waiting with a new creation for him to try. Lemon beurre blanc. A stuffing of smoked trout and goat cheese for taquitos. Halibut in a ginger–orange broth. Adair was confused. How had this teenager learned the techniques that allowed him to achieve such results? Back then, there were no YouTube tutorials available for quick study. Not just a tasty broth, but a clear one! Not just a smoked piece of fish, but one that remained moist yet firm. Half of the time, Adair, the culinary grad, found himself learning from Lalo, who was executing advanced techniques without knowing their proper names.

"I told him at the time, 'Dude, you're like Escoffier reincarnate,' because he had skills, inherited skills. Things he just felt inside of him when it came to food."

Lalo didn't yet understand the reference, but when Adair invoked Escoffier, he was giving out the highest compliment imaginable to a budding cook. Auguste Escoffier, a Frenchman, transformed fine dining during his time, from the mid-nineteenth to the mid-twentieth century. He was called "the king of chefs and the chef of kings." Born to a blacksmith, he rose to prominence at the Savoy Hotel and then helped to launch the Paris Ritz and the Carlton in London. Escoffier is largely responsible for how we conceive of chefs today, creating the *brigade de cuisine* working method, in which cooks dedicate themselves to particular stations under a hierarchy that ascends to the executive chef. He turned the once menial job of cooking into a profession of trained experts.

They had worked together for about two years when Adair began to sense that Lalo was outgrowing his mentorship. To Adair, Lalo was like a captured bird throwing himself against a too-small cage. When Lalo moved on, Adair wasn't angry, just melancholy. After years of camaraderie, he felt the emptiness of losing a good friend.

A job came up at the newly opened Brasserie Le Coze, a restaurant headed by young chef Eric Ripert, born in France and raised in Andorra, who had already made his name in the U.S. for sublime, seafood-focused French cuisine at Le Bernardin in New York City. Lalo walked in with confidence; he was Fast Eddie. Maybe he didn't yet know how to bone a duck, but he could outwork anyone.

Staffing one of Ripert's kitchens granted him admission to a higher echelon of the restaurant world, one that could lead to a professional future he had yet to envision. Here, diners paid handsomely for perfectly executed rack of lamb with ratatouille, and roasted skate wing with braised endive and potatoes in a brown butter caper sauce. At the Georgia Grille, Lalo had made sauces from a few simple ingredients, some of them poured out of cans or cartons. The breakfasts he catered with Adair had included rolls and jugs of orange juice from the supermarket. There was no shame in it; customers were satisfied, and so were his employers.

When Lalo started at Brasserie Le Coze, he had a new language to learn: julienne, mise en place, bouquet garni, and the dozens of other French terms that form the basis of communication in the world of fine dining. What's more, he had to perfect the techniques they signified. He was still learning English, a process that gained horsepower as he spent less time with his family and more with his coworkers.

Ripert's main commitment was to Le Bernardin, so he only made it to Atlanta periodically. But the handful of encounters they shared left a deep mark on the teenage Lalo, who watched as this elegant young Frenchman walked through the door wearing shiny black shoes and a suit, then disappeared into the office to take meetings, only to reemerge dressed in an impeccably white chef's jacket. Ripert spoke to him in Spanish and personally taught him to make potato puree and gazpacho, which would be part of a tasting menu they'd prepare for 150 people—the first tasting menu Lalo had ever witnessed. More than twenty years later, he could still recall the courses with precision: green salad, live scallop crudo, gazpacho, stuffed quail with mushrooms and potato puree, lamb shank with flageolet beans, and fondant with vanilla ice cream for dessert. As Lalo remembers it, when the meal was over, Ripert introduced him to the dining room, where his work was applauded—another first for someone who'd never been in a school play or had his name read from the honor roll.

Afterward, Lalo did what he did most nights. He went home to his family's two-bedroom apartment on Buford Highway with a big bag of potato chips and a couple bottles of Snapple. He sat outside in the dark eating before tiptoeing through the living room where his parents slept and into the bedroom he shared with a cousin, his brother Jaime, and his sister Isela. The other bedroom was used by Maria and her husband, whom she'd met in the Vidalia onion fields years before, and their baby, Antonio.

Lalo tried to spend as little time as possible inside the crowded apartment, which was filled with every variety of sound and smell, from a crying infant to dirty socks, to Natalia's cooking, to arguments between Maria and her husband. "I didn't really belong anywhere. I didn't belong with the people I worked with and I didn't belong with the people I hung out with, and I didn't belong in my house." He fantasized about the different lives he might lead. Later, when he tried to remember his youth, he found it hard to sort reality from this intricately detailed reverie.

There were stories magnetic enough to anchor Lalo in a time and place: when his father's appendix burst, when he shot the deer and brought it home on his shoulders, when the doctor misdiagnosed his mother with cancer. But more often, when he looked back at his life, Lalo felt disoriented—it had all happened so fast, in so many different locations. He struggled to harness his memories and tether them to a timeline.

Lalo began and ended each day with extremes. At school, he'd been held back three times, which meant that boys in his classes still spoke an octave higher and hadn't sprouted chest hair. In the afternoon, he went to work with adults like Adair, more than twice his age. From the time he was five, when he'd used his earnings to buy ice cream for his siblings, he had fashioned himself the man of the house, a leader for his family during Lupe's long absences. But to grow up, he knew he had to do more than impress a room of fancy people. His body twitched with the desire to do that something more, and yet, he had no idea what it was.

CHAPTER THREE

MUSTANG

WHEN HE DIDN'T have work after school, Lalo made a habit of riding the bus to a Ford dealership in the northern Atlanta suburbs. He looked for salesmen who would answer his questions about acceleration rates and the cost of leather interiors. Seeing him coming—a blustery teenager—they practically ducked behind fenders. Who was this skinny kid with wisps of facial hair, telling them in broken English that he was interested in buying a brand-new Mustang? Was he even old enough to drive?

Lalo had a blue 1985 Z28 Camaro that he repainted pistachio green, but after he sold it to his uncle he began to lobby for the '94 Mustang in earnest. He wanted more than a set of wheels—he wanted shock and awe. As an adolescent boy, that meant the kind of car he'd seen in rap videos, the kind of car no one his age was supposed to have in real life.

Lalo had been working for nearly a decade of his young life. In Atlanta, he hustled between jobs at the Georgia Grille and Brasserie Le Coze, school and home. On the road, he'd worked like an adult, but his parents' eyes had been on him at all times, anxiously keeping track of his safety. Now that they were settled in a single place, a new side of him, a hormone-soaked teenager hungry for rebellion, began to raise its voice. After bouncing between schools for years, he was desperate to find a group of peers. He pictured himself as a wolf cub in search of his pack.

The first time his older cousins and their crew invited Lalo to join them for a joyride he immediately said yes, despite being feverish with a bad case of the flu. He boarded their van, then watched as a kid jumped out, stole a car, then used it to run over mailboxes in a suburban neighborhood. The group challenged Lalo that night—how was he going to prove himself? Too sick to do much, Lalo kept his head down, but a few weeks later he experimented with breaking the law, stealing the stereo from a car; it made him giddy. Adair, whose hopes for Lalo's cooking career were already high, grew frustrated. "Don't be just like everyone else," Adair told him. "You're too good for that!"

Lalo was caught stealing stereos two times, and charged with a felony on both occasions. The second time he was caught, he had had the audacity to attempt the crime in a school parking lot. A security guard saw him in the act and quickly called the cops. Lalo was sentenced to four years of intensive probation, requiring him to be supervised and report weekly to a probation officer. Unchastened, he took up a side gig of selling cocaine in the bathroom of a dive bar along Buford Highway, and to his coworkers in kitchens—though he found watching them get high a sad spectacle and was never tempted to try it himself.

Lalo was making a thousand dollars a week. He handed over his legitimate money to Lupe and kept his extracurricular earnings to himself, spending on clothes, music, gas, and the occasional blunt. The campaign for the dream car went on for months. He'd catch Lupe's ear at dinner, pleading: he had worked for the car, it was rightfully his. Later, he'd threaten: he'd find some other way to get the Mustang, someone else to lend him the money and sign the contract. Lupe could have said no. And he did, every day. Lalo was too young for such a car! It would attract the wrong attention. It was *demasiado*—simply too much. Teenage Lalo was by turns cocky, infuriating, charming, insulting, funny. His relationship with his father was defined by conflict—daily skirmishes over Lalo getting home later than he'd promised, hanging out with kids his father didn't approve of, suspicions over drugs. But Lalo was unfailingly loyal and hardworking: he handed over his money faithfully to Lupe each week and never complained about work. Lalo had named one thing he wanted, something he'd quite literally earned. As much as he might have wanted to dismiss the car as a wild indulgence and a liability in their neighborhood, Lupe contended with the request seriously. They'd made it here, to a place where such a purchase was at last possible. Wasn't that something to celebrate?

When he finally caved, Lupe, who lacked credit history, had to ask a woman he cleaned office buildings for some nights to cosign the contract. At the dealership, they shook hands with the salesman, but Lalo didn't get to drive the car home—the woman who cosigned did. Sitting in the backseat, he inhaled the mixture of leather and offgassing chemicals, that new car smell. A '94 white Mustang 5.0! When they reached their apartment, Lupe couldn't summon the will to celebrate. He sat on the front stoop alone and took out his cigarettes, which he kept on hand only for when he had a drink or a moment of high anxiety. He stared over his shoulder at the garage door. It might as well have been a twenty-foot-long fish tank holding a single great white shark.

Inside, Lalo lay on his bed thinking about what the car would mean. *I'm a badass.* At work he'd have better wheels than people three times his age. Better than his boss. *I'm the king of the jungle.*

Lupe had his reasons for saying yes. He and Natalia hadn't put money into a college fund. They knew Lalo's childhood ping-ponging across the South and the Midwest had left him with no hope of such a future. But that didn't mean they weren't proud. They had stable jobs in this new city. Many of their siblings had made the journey to the U.S. and were slowly building businesses. After decades of buying only the absolute necessities and saving the rest, there was finally cash to spare. And when you had money, why shouldn't you spend it? You could deny someone papers, you could deport them, hurl racial slurs. But all dollars being equal, Lupe could walk in and buy a car, same as anyone. Lalo should have that car. He had earned every dime.

For months Lalo would be banned from driving the car—in the frenzy of excitement over his expensive new toy, Lupe didn't trust Lalo to play with it responsibly. Lalo continued to hand over his checks and Lupe used them to make the $890 monthly payment. When Lupe finally gave him the OK to drive the Mustang, there were restrictions: he was only allowed to use it to go to and from work, and not too late at night. Nevertheless, Lalo took the car cruising through downtown Atlanta, and watched heads turn. Before 1994, Mustangs were boxy and square, but that year their hard lines were smoothed into curves. When people saw the car, it was like they were watching the future roll by, with teenage Lalo at the wheel. First, he'd drive through Chamblee, through the newly booming immigrant neighborhood on Buford Highway. Then he'd drive into downtown Atlanta, its heart beating with new money; the Mustang fit right in. The car became the strongest drug in his life. He got high off the car's power and sexy curves, and blasted Tupac, Kid Frost, and Tha

Mexakinz from its speakers. When he saw how his crush admired the car, he made sure he was available to drive her wherever she needed to go.

———

Even after victoriously convincing Lupe to buy the Mustang, eighteen-year-old Lalo chafed at how difficult it still was to get Lupe to part with a few bucks for clothes or food or gas. He watched the diners at Brasserie Le Coze enjoy refined meals, and the drug kingpins in his neighborhood wear fly clothes. His appreciation for money only intensified: who it could impress, where it could take you. He hated begging Lupe for money that should have been his. So, when his friends told him about their grand idea to rob the S–S Bottle Shop on Peachtree Road, Lalo immersed himself in the plot. It was the check-cashing hub for the neighborhood, and they expected the till would be full.

They arrived late in the morning on a Friday at the end of March. Lalo waited in the driver's seat, a few hundred meters from the liquor store in the parking lot of a barbecue joint. When his friends ran out of the liquor store, Lalo looked out the driver's side window at the shock of fresh blood on their clothes and faces. They slammed the doors shut and Lalo pulled onto Peachtree Road, driving a mile to the apartment complex where his friends lived, going the speed limit. They hid inside the apartment and listened to the slam of the patrol car door as two cops got out and began making the rounds. When it was their turn—*tap tap tap*—his friend's girlfriend opened the door, nonchalant: Nah, no one's here. The cops continued on. But it was clear that this wasn't over. Short of a Lamborghini or the Batmobile, his car was the most ostentatious choice possible for a crime that depended on ducking under the radar. And it's not like he was far from home—he was in his own neighborhood, driving the car that everyone from gangs to cops had whistled at since he first brought it back from the dealership. There were plenty of witnesses as his friends ran out of the store, plenty of time to take down the license plate number and call the police. Soon, the Mustang would be found where Lalo had abandoned it, and the registration would lead them right back to Lupe at the family apartment on Coronado Place, just two miles from the crime scene. It was like they'd made a run at the school principal's wallet on a Tuesday at 10 a.m., yelling their own names as they retreated.

Lalo had been caught before, but he'd managed to avoid jail time. The stereos and bags of coke seemed like victimless crimes to his teenage brain. The blood told another story. Later, when Lalo and his friends decided to make a run for it to Mexico, he'd learn what had happened in the liquor store. They'd demanded the money. To their surprise, the cashier, Jung Ho Kim, refused. They pistol-whipped him in the forehead and tried to drag him to the cooler at the back of the store, then get to the register, but he continued to fight back and eventually ran out into the street, bleeding and screaming frantically for help. They ran to the Mustang, their pockets empty.

Lalo waited at his friend's apartment for a couple of hours before leaving for his shift at the Georgia Grille. Detectives confronted him there at 8:30 that evening. "At first," the detective wrote in his report, "Garcia claimed that he went to work at 9 a.m. that day and someone stole his car. He then admitted that he had loaned it to someone named Rodriguez. He then stated that Christopher borrowed the car. Garcia advised that he would provide us with more information as he discovered it." After sweating through the rest of his shift, Lalo went to a bar and met up with his accomplices. It was Friday—payday—and he cashed his checks. It seemed like only a matter of

time before his story was untangled. The friends, who all had roots in
Mexico, drove the 1,100 miles to Laredo, through the night and most
of the following day. Lalo's head was swimming with the imagined
admonishments of Lupe and Natalia. What were you thinking? After
all we sacrificed for you? Didn't we warn you about hanging out with
people like that? Didn't we teach you to be a better man than this?

At the border, his friends went into a convenience store and tried
to buy supplies with one of Lalo's hundred-dollar bills. They came
back outside to inform him that the cashier had rejected the bill as
counterfeit. "Wait here," they told Lalo. "We're going to change some
more money, and we'll be back." An hour passed as he slowly realized
what had happened: they'd taken most of his money and left him, the
liability who'd talked to the cops, at the border. With the hundred-
dollar bill that remained in his pocket, Lalo bought tickets at the bus
station, with transfers in Monterrey and San Luis Potosí before he
made it to his village in Guanajuato.

In the intervening day and a half, Lupe and Natalia had been
in a panic. They were visited by the detectives when Lalo didn't
show up for work, but the story the cops told made no sense. How
could Lalo have pistol-whipped a store clerk? There must be some
mistake.

Lalo got off the bus and continued on to his grandfather's house,
a simple adobe building with goats, chickens, and pigs in pens just
outside the door of the living room. Lalo hadn't been to his village
in a decade and his grandfather was mired in gambling debt. The
small businesses they once operated were gone now, and in the years
since Lupe had departed, so too had scores of customers they had
once served; like him they'd left to find their fortune elsewhere.
Now, those who remained depended on their land and remittances
for survival.

Lalo called home and Natalia answered—sad, furious, sick with worry.

Que hiciste? What did you do?

Yo no hice nada! Lalo insisted. I didn't do anything.

You put us in danger, Natalia told him. Stay where you are.

Lalo spent the next two months in relative isolation, speaking little, caring for the animals, and sleeping on a bed of corn husks, like he had as a boy. From a bird's eye view, it seemed like Lalo was moving between extremes: working for one of the most famous chefs on the planet and driving a new Mustang, to shoveling manure in the town that his parents had left for lack of opportunity. But Lalo, who had spent his formative years compelled to eschew attachments to homes, schools, and friends as he moved from place to place, took the change in stride. This was the village that had captured his heart as a child, the place he always left unwillingly. What he longed for was the blanket of familial approval that had always kept him warm. In his absence, Natalia, Lupe, and his siblings had come to an implicit agreement: it was simply implausible that Lalo had anything to do with the crime. Obviously, he had fallen on a sword, in keeping with the sacrificing temperament that had characterized his childhood, the kid all too eager to take on the responsibilities of adults even when he wasn't asked. In a couple of months, Lupe wired money to Mexico and Lalo said goodbye to his grandparents and his village, unsure when they'd see each other again.

Lalo was able to make it back across the border in a taxi, in the days when a passport wasn't required for entry. He returned to Brasserie Le Coze and the Georgia Grille with his tail between his legs, and assured his managers that the previous month's absence had been a misunderstanding. They received him easily; it was difficult to come by workers like Lalo, who competed with themselves toward an impossible standard. Natalia and Lupe continued on in a state of denial.

Time seemed to trickle by. Lalo was impatient to be caught. When the manager of the Georgia Grille finally told him that the police had called, he was relieved. He finished the shift, walked to a payphone, and called the detective back. "Turn yourself in," said the voice on the other end of the line. "If you do, I can help you." Lalo got the sense that they were desperate to rubber-stamp the casefile CLOSED; if he'd go along and accept blame for everything, he was likely to get a lighter sentence.

CHAPTER FOUR

RAMEN WITH DORITOS

AT THE FRANK SCOTT State Prison in Hardwick, Georgia, Lalo started his day with a breakfast of gluey grits, burnt coffee, and pale powdered eggs, then stripped naked so he could be searched before boarding a bus in his blue and white Georgia State Penitentiary Uniform. Lalo cut grass, like his father, a hundred miles away—only the lawns Lalo trimmed surrounded government-owned hospitals and office buildings, while Lupe worked the acres of a country club in Alpharetta. Lalo ate his state-provided lunches of mystery meat and powdered drink, and while no one had a smile for the inmates landscaping under the pitiless sun, work remained his comfort zone. He found reassurance in the act of walking out of his cell, completing a task, and returning physically spent. The strip searches became routine, but remained degrading.

After Lalo turned himself in, he had been locked up in county jail. Charged with aggravated assault, he was put in a section with others accused of violent crimes. The first night, no bed available, he tucked his arms inside his newly-issued jumpsuit and curled up on the floor. It was freezing. His skull throbbed with constant noise: doors opening and closing, shouting, the whoosh of the air conditioning. Lalo would stay there for eight months, awaiting his hearing. He hired the only lawyer he knew of, Luzmina Gonzalez, whose name he'd heard around his neighborhood. Finally, she got him out on bond and he spent a few months waiting for his court date. In that time Gonzalez was able to work out a plea deal: he could either go to prison for three years for aggravated assault—a felony—or he could go on trial and risk thirty. Either way, he'd likely be deported at the end of his sentence. He took the plea, one count of aggravated assault.

In the courtroom, Lalo stood alone next to his attorney. Before he was sentenced, the judge offered him the chance to make a statement—this was his moment to ask for leniency and throw himself on the mercy of the court. "He wanted me to say, 'I don't deserve to go to jail, I've been working all my life. I come from a very good family, I need a break. Just this one time, I need a break and you'll never hear from me again.' That's what he wanted me to say, I know this." Instead, Lalo stayed quiet. He'd never been one to look for an easy way out. Sometimes, that ferocity of endurance had translated into wrapping his finger and covering it with a latex glove to keep his blood from contaminating the diners' food as he continued on with his shift. Now, it meant admitting he'd done something wrong and agreeing to the punishment, even if it met someone else's crime. Lupe and Natalia refused to acknowledge that Lalo had been involved in the robbery turned assault. They didn't attend the hearing.

That day, when the judge asked him to speak, Lalo gazed back, silent. He was sentenced to three years minus the eight months he'd served—months he'd spent dreading this moment, inventing doomsday scenarios of twenty, thirty years behind bars. But seeing

no familiar faces in the courtroom, Lalo had a last request: he wanted
to go home and say goodbye to his family.

The judge gave Lalo the weekend. He walked out of the courtroom, his face set and determined, his eyes leaking tears. At home,
Lupe pressed him. He still couldn't believe his son bore responsibility for the crime. I don't want to run from this my whole life, Lalo
told him.

The offer that came next was bigger than the Mustang: Lupe
would uproot the whole family and they would return to Mexico
together. *Es eso lo que quieres?* Lupe asked. Is that what you want?
They would remain unified and Lalo could avoid prison. They had
the house in the Estado de México, some extended family, some savings. No, Lalo said. He wouldn't be responsible for stripping his family of the life they'd made, every detail of which they'd paid for a
hundred times above the asking price.

Once he'd settled at the medium security prison, Lalo turned
to an unlikely source of comfort: reading. Though he'd struggled in
school to attain basic literacy, here he was denied everything except
time and library access. While his peers from high school were out
working in the free world or attending college classes, Lalo borrowed
books from the prison library, lay on his twin-size bed on top of a
state-issued blanket, and slogged through words that turned into
sentences and paragraphs.

During the week, he organized his time as a means of self-
preservation. When faced in full, any one day was too long to survive, but if he focused on the allotment of time for breakfast, work,
showering, dinner, reading, or bed, he could make it through each
increment and to the other side.

He read dozens of westerns by Louis L'Amour, propulsive stories
of cowboys overcoming obstacles, rewarded for their trials with love

and fortune. In the romance novels of Danielle Steel, the language was clean and visual, a perfect teaching tool: "three daisies bobbed in a glass, and the bread was fresh and soft to the touch." And you could always find at least one copy of *National Geographic* in his cell. He'd rip out his favorite photographs and keep them tucked in a notebook, saving them for dark moments when he might dive out of the gray walls and swim along the coral reefs of the Indian Ocean.

The first year of his sentence was studiously unremarkable. The energetic showoff who had rolled around town in a Mustang was forced to do his best impersonation of a ghost, to float through the state prison unnoticed. Years later, he would wonder if this shift might have been a natural maturation that simply took place against an unusual backdrop: teenagers mellow out eventually, and Lalo was heading into his twenties.

After that year came a change, as the first steps of an administrative process were taken to deport Lalo at the end of his sentence. This meant a transfer to a maximum security prison in Glennville, Georgia, and a shocked Lalo was shackled and put on a bus. Before he left, his bunkmate offered some advice: the minute you arrive, find some friends. Sure enough, two classmates from high school were in the same prison, and Lalo found safety in their company.

Smith's State was more than a cut below previous conditions, but Lalo had spent nearly two years in training, between his time awaiting trial in county jail and his first year in prison. For one thing, he had learned that it helped to shut away memories of the outside. Even so, Lalo couldn't help but "cook." He'd save a hard-boiled egg and a mayonnaise packet from breakfast and make egg salad as an afternoon snack. Or he'd prepare his signature prison dish: ramen noodles with Doritos on top. Ingredients: one packet ramen noodles, hot water, one small bag of Doritos (or other chips). With the package still closed, smash the ramen noodles against a hard surface. Pour into a bowl and add just enough hot water to submerge the noodles. Cover the bowl and wait 10 minutes. Now, throw the bag of Doritos against a hard surface several times until they're broken into small, fluorescent splinters. Uncover the ramen and sprinkle the Doritos on top. Don't expect much. Don't think about the food you used to eat, the tasting menu you once cooked with Eric Ripert, your father's flour tortillas, your mother's tamales. Just eat your neon slop and be glad your family put money in the commissary. Feeds one.

Despite his best efforts, for five minutes of every day nostalgia for that life tore through his body, demanding to be acknowledged. It seemed to happen most often at lights out, when he fell into the trap that his own mind had stealthily set. It was then that he thought of the same meditative hour in his family home. The warmth of his mother's cooking still lingered in the air, her hands plunged into the hot, soapy water in the kitchen sink. Maria would be pulling into the parking lot soon after her restaurant shift, her son Antonio stealing a last bit of TV before he was tucked into bed. Lupe was next to him on the couch, the smell of cut grass clinging to his skin. Then Lalo jolted himself back to reality. The comfort of his family, of his home, drained from his body. Time stretched out before him and he felt its weight like black earth on his chest. He tried to summon sleep to dispose of a few more hours. But even sleep seemed to be wasted when he was saving his energy for another day in this place. As a free person, sleep was nourishment, fuel for all he might pursue in his free life. In prison, those hours were only spent waiting for life to begin again. He worked, read, showered, watched TV, ate his meals, went to sleep. He kept his distance from the other incarcerated men. "You see guys have nervous breakdowns, you see guys commit suicide, you see guys get into fights to go to the hole so they can be alone." Someone would disappear and no one knew where they'd been taken. Lalo didn't ask. "You do your own time."

Lalo knew that many of the men he was incarcerated alongside would get out one day and just as soon end up back in the same beds, eating the same mystery meat and off-brand powdered drink. There was nothing inside that resembled an effort to rehabilitate them. In fact, Lalo's time coincided with the reign of Wayne Garner, a famously merciless Georgia corrections commissioner who systematically removed anything he perceived as bells and whistles—including academic and vocational teaching—from the state's prisons as he presided over violent shakedowns of incarcerated men by guards dressed all in black.

As the days crept by, Lalo began to reevaluate his path. Outside, his work at the Georgia Grille and even Brasserie Le Coze had seemed to be little more than gussied-up labor for hire. He performed a series of tasks and in exchange got paid. When he was working for Eric Ripert, he was intrigued by his elegant boss, the same way he might have been had he worked craft services on a movie set and caught sight of a famous actor. But he hadn't yet begun to consider where cooking might take him, the deeper concepts he might learn from such a chef. In prison, he began to wonder what heights he might achieve if he gave cooking his whole heart.

And he wondered what might have happened if Lupe had refused him the Mustang. It was a potent symbol of his worst self, his greed and arrogance, a first domino that sent the rest crashing down. But seen in a different light, it was a symbol of how hard the family had worked, of how much his father cared for him. The more he thought about it, the more certain he became that the car had nothing to do with his fate. He had always been determined to push the limits: competition with people twice his age, egging his siblings on until his parents yelled, working double shifts, chopping faster until there was blood on the cutting board. He was certain that he would have continued to test authority until he met a consequence significant enough to stop him in his tracks. He was grateful he'd never cut off a digit, and that his crimes hadn't yielded a still graver result.

Two months before Lalo expected to complete his sentence, he got word that he was to be transported again, this time to an immigration detention center. Lalo looked at the judge through a video monitor. Were his parents U.S. citizens? No. Neither Lupe nor Natalia had wanted to change their status from permanent residents to citizens—they hadn't seen the point. Perfect, the judge said, no holdup. The deportation would move forward.

Lupe and Natalia knew what could happen if Lalo were dumped in Nuevo Laredo by the Border Patrol bus: he was a prime kidnapping target, easy pickings for extortion by a gang, or worse. Maria and her husband drove to meet Lalo at the release point, picked him up, and headed south to San José de las Pilas. Yet again, Lalo used his grandparents' house as a refuge. But this time he wasn't running; he was free. He could spend all day outside. He could breathe clean air and go where he pleased. As it turned out, Lalo didn't have much time to decide if he'd be contented with life in Mexico. Just a few weeks after he arrived, Natalia called with grave news. Lupe had been feeling some pain in his stomach after meals and the doctors were worried. Would Lalo come home? Yes, he told them. Yes.

CHAPTER FIVE

THE GOLDEN CAGE

BEFORE LALO WAS incarcerated, he and his family were living in Chamblee. Lalo was still a teenager and Lupe was healthy. Now, his family owned a house in the quiet suburb of Alpharetta, twenty miles away, close to Lupe's landscaping job. Whereas Chamblee was a bustling immigrant hub, Alpharetta was rural, predominantly middle-class and white. They'd sold the Mustang to help with the down payment.

Lupe was fifty-three. Working on the golf course daily had kept him strong. But when rumbles turned to sharp stomach pains after meals, he went to his doctor. A camera was guided down his throat into his stomach and spotted the clenched fist of a tumor. Stage four. That's what Dr. Christopher Hart told Lupe and Natalia in the quiet of his office. Surgery, chemo, and radiation could buy Lupe a few months, perhaps a year to live. There was no cure.

They didn't talk about the pesticides then, which had been on their hands, their clothes, in their lungs, and on their food in the fields. It wasn't until later, when other friends and family who had dedicated themselves to picking crops started to die young, that they began to name the cause of death. The link between pesticide exposure and premature death has been difficult to prove. Migrant field workers, traveling from crop to crop, are exposed to many chemicals, frustrating attempts to pinpoint a specific culprit and force accountability. And because of the constant moving around, it becomes difficult to identify a disease cluster, which might manifest years or decades after exposure.

During those months of treatment, Lalo and Lupe shuffled into the car at 5 a.m. and drove silently to Emory University Hospital. Lupe didn't like to talk during the treatments; he'd just sit under a thick wool blanket and absentmindedly watch the TV screens around the room. The conflict that had defined his relationship with adolescent Lalo had evaporated. Life was precious; they savored their togetherness.

Over his decades in the fields, Lupe had leaned on his Catholic faith, at times the only thing that held him up. The Garcías didn't say grace before meals or pray at bedtime. But God was close to Lupe's heart, a private matter that he invoked every time he got into a car and thanked the Virgencita *por este día*. Again, she was there for him in his darkest hour.

Lupe had health insurance, thanks to his job at the country club, but Lalo felt more pressure than ever to provide for his family. He briefly worked with Jaime, making door panels at a GMC car plant, but he couldn't stand the robotic work. He decided to find another restaurant; without the Mustang or a driver's license, he set off on foot.

When Lalo was cooking at Brasserie Le Coze, his colleagues sometimes read the restaurant reviews in the *Atlanta Journal–Constitution*. Unable to fathom the influence a single chef might exert on society, Lalo was perplexed and intrigued by the effort and analysis that went into writing about food. John Kessler was the paper's dining critic, and when he was seated at one of their tables, the level of crazy in the kitchen cranked up to an eleven.

It was during that time that Lalo had heard about a fine dining restaurant in Roswell, a nearby suburb, called Van Gogh's. It was headed by Michele and Chris Sedgwick, a young couple who had built their small restaurant group from nothing. Van Gogh's, which they opened with $8,000, was their first venture. Soon enough, Michele said, "we were really crazy successful, we were doing three and a half million dollars a year." Both cooked and brought their distinct talents to the table: Chris was the big-picture guy, who dreamed up concepts and pulled together the funding, staff, equipment, and space. Michele, a recent culinary school grad, was the details person, immersed in the minutiae—presentation, hospitality, and decor—that makes a good dining experience great. Together, they created the menu.

During those years in prison, the name Van Gogh's had stuck in Lalo's mind, along with Kessler's glowing review. But he didn't actively seek out a job in the kitchen. Rather, after a couple of short stints at some ill-fated restaurants within walking distance of his family's new Alpharetta home, he tried another spot accessible by foot: Vinny's on Windward.

Vinny's also belonged to the Sedgwicks, and was inspired by interpretations of Italian food in the Napa Valley. In the Atlanta suburbs, it was difficult to find spaces with character, so they'd brought in stately wood doors and antique brick. The archways and crawling ivy brought to mind a university campus or a monastery. When Lalo walked into Vinny's, he had no idea that it was owned by the same couple as Van Gogh's.

Lalo hadn't cooked in over three years, but for a twenty-two-year-old, he already had a substantial amount of experience, and the name Eric Ripert made ears perk up. Now that he was living in the country illegally, the familiar work he'd done—dicing vegetables, grilling, sautéing—felt suspect and tense. The kitchen became a stage where Lalo performed select scenes from his former life, surrounded by co-stars who weren't in on the act. Any dissimilarity took on a menacing quality, reminding Lalo that he was trapped in a *Twilight Zone* episode that would likely end with his deportation—only he had no idea whether it would be today or ten years in the future. He was reminded of one of his father's favorite songs, performed by the Tejano band Los Tigres del Norte. It was called "La Jaula de Oro"—The Golden Cage. "What's the money for if I'm like an inmate / inside this great nation? / When I think about it I cry, and even though the bars are gold / it never stops being a prison." Before, he'd cruised through Atlanta blasting music in his showy car, basking in attention. Now, he walked along the suburban roads to work, fearing any passing driver who might stare at him for a moment too long.

Lalo sought to prove himself at Vinny's. He started as a line cook, a lowly position in a fine dining kitchen, but the Sedgwicks were savvy and it didn't take long for them to promote him to sous-chef, the second in command. By then, Lalo had fallen in love, and Chris and Michele invited the couple to their home for what they thought was a party. When Lalo walked through the door, he realized they were the only guests. The Sedgwicks made him an offer: head chef of Van Gogh's. More responsibility, more creative freedom, and a bigger salary. It was a dream opportunity. Lalo went quiet, then told them he'd have to decline. A chef has to make executive decisions: pricing the menu, determining the size of orders, and keeping it all under budget. Lalo explained to the Sedgwicks that he'd been in and out of school as a kid and still struggled with reading and arithmetic. Michele and Chris looked at one another. It was no problem. They'd provide him with an assistant; his job was to create and to cook.

The Sedgwicks were certain they had discovered a diamond in the rough, and they wanted Lalo to sparkle. After his shift, they'd take him to restaurants in downtown Atlanta and analyze everything they saw and tasted. What was new? What was merely trendy? What would endure? When they traveled abroad, they brought back menus, books, and pictures for Lalo to study. These were nice gestures, certainly, but they were more substantive than that: the Sedgwicks believed that Lalo was capable of outcooking any of the food they'd tried, and, ever the competitor, Lalo was emboldened to rise to the challenge.

Van Gogh's had opened at a time when a restaurant's success was increasingly driven by the figurehead of the chef, formerly invisible from the dining room. Now, the chefs were the protagonists, with a growing cohort of food media to build them up. In the past, only a few exceptional chefs, like Alice Waters, Julia Child, and Wolfgang Puck, had become household names in the United States. But now, more and more personalities were gaining notice across the country, and diners were traveling long distances and spending lavishly to eat in their restaurants. In the Napa Valley, Thomas Keller's star was rising at the French Laundry, along with his philosophy of hyper-local food; in Chicago, at WD-50, Wylie Dufresne had turned the role of chef into something between a cook and a mad scientist, a style dubbed molecular gastronomy. Michele was searching for the person who would transform Van Gogh's, which was not nearly as creative a spot as its name aspired to. While their regular customer base was satisfied, the Sedgwicks wanted their flagship property to gain accolades, stay ahead of trends, and create a buzz in a city not yet regarded as a culinary destination. Michele had given previous chefs the liberty of devising a few specials, trying to see what they were capable of, but she was alternately annoyed, disappointed, and horrified by the results. Then came Lalo, who began to put together flavors in an intelligent way. He absorbed her insights, and they could talk about innovative approaches; those discussions began to feel like collaboration. Two people with a similar vision. Two people aspiring to a level of excellence they hadn't achieved before.

Then, on Valentine's Day, Chris gave Lalo the chance to create his own menu. When February 15 rolled around, he could see that Lalo was dejected as he returned to the usual.

Just write a different menu every day, Chris said, casually handing off an outlandish amount of power to a young cook who had been working for him for less than a year. Lalo grabbed the baton and never looked back. "It was a shit show," Michele said, but a fun one. She loved getting caught in the tornado of Lalo's creativity and being swept away.

In every other corner of his life, Lalo was walking a tightrope. He constantly anticipated the day the whole thing would come crashing down: his immigration status would be discovered, his father's cancer would come to its predictable end. In the kitchen, however, the Sedgwicks had given him complete freedom. Some days, he could exchange his anxieties for the dizzying pressure of the dinner rush. At other times, he redirected his agitation at lower-stakes targets, like an improperly seared scallop or a late employee. He became a temperamental diva, exuberant, full of demands.

Authoring a daily menu meant that these demands were in constant flux. While a fixed menu allowed the kitchen to establish a dependable system for preparing the components of each dish before the frenzy of service began, the inevitable setbacks of making untested dishes siphoned off precious time, until the kitchen degenerated into barely-controlled chaos.

Ten minutes before service, Lalo would put in a call to Michele at home. "I need you to go to Whole Foods for me to get chanterelles," he'd say.

"No fucking way! I'm waiting for my daughter to get home."

"So wait for her, take her, and get me my chanterelles."

Michele would arrive, throw the bag of mushrooms at him, and walk out. Then the menu could at last be printed, moments before service. Despite the headaches, Michele was thrilled at the restaurant's transformation.

Lalo had been given permission to invent, but that didn't mean he had anything particularly original to contribute. He'd gone from prepping other cooks' recipes to conceiving of the occasional dish, to being in charge of a constantly changing menu. When he said that something looked good, he meant it literally. He'd see a photo online and read a description, then get into the kitchen and test out different versions until he settled on the one he liked.

Lalo especially admired Rick Bayless, the chef who had lived in Mexico in the 1980s and found fame in Chicago with his PBS series *Cooking Mexican*, and his restaurants Topolobampo and Frontera Grill. Many Americans learned to make Mexican food from Bayless. Lalo was inspired by the way Bayless approached Mexican cooking: committed to learning about regional techniques and dishes as they were prepared in Mexico, yet open to the possibility of innovation. But Lalo also felt ashamed that it had taken a non-Mexican for his country's food to become respected in the United States.

Slowly, Lalo began to innovate. Many of these attempts went into the trash, along with the money the Sedgwicks were spending to fund his self-education. Luckily for Lalo, Michele had had a similar experience at the start of her career, when she was hired as a pastry chef in the late 1980s at the Atlanta-area Country Club of the South. She arrived for her first day of work with just two weeks of pastry training at culinary school. With no one paying any attention, she taught herself.

Most of the flavors from Lalo's childhood—epazote, black beans, moronga—didn't make it onto the plate at Van Gogh's, but there were exceptions: a gazpacho with crab ceviche nestled in the center of the bowl, tuna tartare with ginger and soy served on a bed of avocado relish. "The blend of textures and flavors is stellar," said one reviewer. Sometimes he struck out: a lime crème brûlée in a mango soup was a chaotic mix of competing flavors, and the slice of tofu garnishing a confit of pheasant and pheasant breast "an altogether too-far-afield garnish." When Lalo made European classics, he depended on Michele's worldly palate to pronounce whether he'd gotten them right.

Lalo enjoyed the freedom that the Sedgwicks offered him, but it was Michele's way of cooking and eating that left the longest-lasting impact. She counted Judy Rodgers of San Francisco's Zuni Café as an inspiration, and taught Lalo about the sophistication of beautifully made simple food, what in restaurant parlance was called rustic. She'd butter a slice of sourdough bread, its interior chewy and supple, its crust subtly caramelized, then slide a runny egg on top. Such a dish embodied the divine union that occurs when simplicity meets perfect execution and perfect execution meets the best quality ingredients. Then she'd tell Lalo, "Taste." It was part command, part enticement.

From Chris, Lalo learned about the importance of coaching potential leaders within a team—making the best of your staff into partners, so that as business grew, you could count on the people you'd put in charge. And by putting so much power into Lalo's hands so early, the couple taught him that you had to go with your gut and take chances.

The diners at Van Gogh's weren't necessarily thrilled with the changes. What had worked for years—mounds of food, a walk-in packed with cream and butter, piles of julienned vegetables—now felt needlessly heavy and dated, like a dowdy valance weighing down a set of lithe silk drapes. The Sedgwicks were prepared to bid adieu to some of their clients, along with the style they adored, in hopes of finding a new audience and remaining relevant.

Lalo was still with the woman whom he'd brought to the Sedg-wicks' house, and soon she'd give birth to their son, Max. The child's arrival was a joyful bit of news that pleased no one more than Lupe. Max was a happy baby whom Natalia cared for while his father worked and his mother attended classes.

Lupe had surprised Dr. Hart with how well he responded to treatment, though he was never declared cancer-free. He spent time with Max and the family, and Lalo cooked for him on occasion, mainly on holidays. Once, Lalo prepared roasted quail, potato puree, and jus. Lupe returned for seconds, thirds, fourths. But with a stage four diagnosis, the good times couldn't last. In 2005, Lupe came back to Dr. Hart with a blockage; there was another tumor, this time in his small intestine.

Lalo took shelter in the restaurant. His relationships there deep-ened. He came to see the staff as a second family, the restaurant as a second home, a place to escape from the devastating scene in his parents' house as his family helplessly watched Lupe deteriorate. But even at work, the comfort he sought was undermined by the pos-sibility of deportation that lurked around every corner. Who would betray him? The parents of Max's mother, whom he suspected were displeased with her choice of a Mexican man? A rival cook in the restaurant? The husband of a woman with whom he'd had an affair? Each day ricocheted between sensuality, banality, and anxiety.

Lalo engrossed himself in a new project: the Sedgwicks wanted to open a Mexican restaurant in Alpharetta, with Lalo at the helm. It would serve freshly-made salsas, tamales, chilaquiles, enchiladas, and more. The concept was upscale casual, the kind of place where you might grab a bite during the week or take a date on a Saturday night for their bespoke margaritas. PURE Taqueria, as it was called after the gas station it replaced, marked the first time in Lalo's professional life that he was primarily cooking Mexican food, and his mother's lessons about rice and beans, salsa and carnitas could find their way directly to the diners he served. Natalia even made tamales for the menu once a week.

Mexican food had long since permeated other parts of the country. As journalist Gustavo Arellano has written, the cuisine was ravenously devoured in the U.S. for centuries, even as it was mocked and blamed as the source of gastrointestinal turmoil. "People didn't even try to imagine Mexican food as something rarefied, or refined, or even regional for that matter. Mexican food was a monolith," Arellano said. Lalo's uncle Martin García was among those who endeavored to find his fortune north of the border via the cuisine of his homeland. He opened a small eatery called Mi Taco in Marietta in 2001. Soon, he and his wife had saved enough to open a larger restaurant, which they pragmatically named 7 Tequilas—a lucky number, and an identifiably Mexican name. In the early years, he found that his audience craved standards already popular north of the border: enchiladas, burritos, nachos. As time went on and more Atlantans began visiting Mexico and returned home hungry for what they'd tried, the menu changed, the salsas and moles grew more complex, the ingredients more specialized. Those diners have (mostly) moved past the hocus pocus that Mexican food, in and of itself, makes you sick, just two centuries after Louis Pasteur debunked the theory of spontaneous generation. Like so many other successful Mexican restaurateurs, Martin accurately gauged what the public wanted—be it chiles rellenos or bean dip—and delivered.

———

During his final days, Lupe was condemned to a liquid diet, but every Sunday you could find him tending to the grill. When the meat was ready, he'd cut it into ever smaller pieces and quietly sit down to eat. But no matter how minute the slices, no matter how long he chewed, he soon began to choke and gasp for air. Natalia might have scolded him. Instead, she drove him to the hospital, where another emergency endoscopy cleared out the blockage, and gave thanks for another week.

On the day Lupe died, Lalo was summoned from work to the hospital. Lupe's last words to Lalo were of a piece with his life, imploring Lalo to care for his family. Jaime had married, had a baby, and moved into his own house. Lalo was now expected to carry the torch, and ensure the welfare of his mother and siblings. When Lupe looked into Lalo's eyes just before he died, Lalo saw everything he needed to know about his father's love.

Having returned to the U.S. illegally after his deportation, Lalo couldn't risk crossing into Mexico to attend Lupe's funeral. It was the greatest indignity of his life as an undocumented man. He helped Natalia make the arrangements for Lupe's frozen body to be flown to Mexico City, but it was Jaime who rode on the plane to assure their father's safe arrival. In San José de las Pilas, neighbors and relatives packed the church. They cooked enough mole and chicken and rice to feed the village, and Natalia looked around in amazement. She'd grown accustomed to the loneliness of finding her way in cities and towns that barely knew she existed. When she went looking for help, when she wept in clinics and asked them to tell her what was wrong, the doctors had little more than Tylenol to offer. Here she was buoyed, understood. No matter her long absence, the shelter of their company was her birthright.

As he grew older, Lalo's love for his father never diminished, but he revered him less. "He wasn't a role model father. But that's what he knew. He didn't do it on purpose. Sometimes I do feel that he had a little bit of resentment, or maybe he's a lot like me where sometimes I'm in such a rage and I don't know why, and I take it out on people. Maybe he had a little bit of that. 'You're gonna work, we're gonna work months without stopping, from when the sun goes up to when the sun goes down.' He comes from a background where that's what he was shown."

Once Lupe was gone, Lalo grew more detached and Natalia was despondent. Each day that Lalo invested in this temporary life felt halfway wasted. He wasn't an engaged father. The businesses he ran didn't belong to him. His relationship with Max's mother was on the rocks.

The scaffolding of routine held him up, but only for so long. When he thought back on those years, the image that stuck out seemed dementedly dull: car key in hand, he'd open the driver's side door each morning, turn the key in the ignition. At the end of the day, he'd turn the key again and start back home. The fact that he could remember the moment when he turned off his car seemed to him an indicator that something was deeply wrong.

That year, the Sedgwicks renamed the restaurant Bistro VG and gave it a thorough makeover. Lalo was interested in the renovation and went with Michele on her trips to buy linens and choose furniture. But his mind was elsewhere. He spent hours fantasizing about getting caught by immigration authorities. A customer would push the door open and the glint of sunshine reflecting off the parking lot caught his peripheral vision, quickening his pulse: Maybe now. Maybe here. Maybe when his hands were slick with fish guts. Maybe when he was sitting with Max at the dinner table on his day off, tucking into a guisado. The agents would haul him away as Natalia stood stock still and Max's trembling face exploded in tears and snot. Getting caught seemed like the only option, and deep down he began to crave the arrival of that moment and the relief it would deliver.

And then the day came. It was 2006. Max was four years old and Lalo had spent seven years living illegally in the U.S. Seven years with his heart in his throat. Seven years a ghost. A pair of plain-clothes customs enforcement agents walked through the entrance of Bistro VG and asked the manager, Jennifer Velazquez, if Lalo was there. They used a last name she didn't recognize, and she told them that no one by that name worked in the restaurant. Then she went back into the kitchen and warned Lalo of their arrival. Jennifer was hysterical; Lalo tried to calm her down as he assessed his surroundings. "I have to see Max," he said. The Sedgwicks were on a ski vacation in Colorado, and as Jennifer picked up the phone to call them, she turned her back to Lalo, wanting to be able to feign ignorance to the agents if he made a run for it.

Behind the restaurant was a small stand of woods; behind that, suburbia. Lalo walked out the back door for a moment, weighing his options, but the restaurant was surrounded. He wouldn't be seeing

Max again. He walked back into the dining room, put his hands out as they were cuffed, and sat down at one of the tables. A familiar flavor imprinted on his palate: bitter relief. "I had plenty of chances, I could have gone anywhere. And I thought about it. But imagine, you're running from what and for what?"

CHAPTER SIX

THE RETURN

In 2007, Lalo returned to Mexico, defeated. Though he had expected this moment for years, it still carried the nauseating stench of failure.

It took a week for the Garcías to track Lalo down after he was taken into custody by ICE. He had been transported to a Georgia detention facility where he spent a few months before signing a waiver on Valentine's Day, pledging that he would never again return to the United States. A rickety plane deposited him in Laredo, where he was sent across the bridge, picked up by family, and driven the thirteen hours south to the Estado de México in silence. "The answers were always in my father's mouth and this time my father wasn't with us."

Natalia decided to stay in Mexico with Lalo for a few months while he began looking for a job. He started the search in Canada, figuring he could earn a good salary to send back to his family in Alpharetta. He found postings on Craigslist for positions across the country, and set up interviews from Prince Edward Island to Vancouver, then bought a multi-destination ticket. But when the plane landed early in the morning in Toronto, four immigration officers awaited Lalo on the jetbridge—he hadn't realized the two countries' immigration authorities shared intelligence.

"They didn't even ask to see my ID. They said, 'Lift up your shirt.' So, I lifted up my shirt and they had a picture of the prison tattoo on my stomach," GARCIA spelled out above his navel in gothic font, two inches tall. "They said, 'Are you Eduardo García?' I said, 'Yes.' They said, 'Step aside.'"

Lalo spent the day at the Toronto airport, where agents sorted through his belongings—some clothes, a toothbrush, and a pile of reviews he'd printed out over the years to show potential employers.

"One of the officers goes, 'It's too bad you can't come into Canada, you seem like a really good guy—I've been reading all your newspaper clippings. But it's just the way it is.'"

Another waiver signed, another flight back to Mexico. The plane sat on the runway for hours while technicians fixed a mechanical issue, and flight attendants tried to keep the passengers happy with free drinks. When they finally took off, the apologetic pilot told them which cluster of light floating in the darkness was Louisville. Lalo said farewell to the places he'd lived, and others he'd never get to know. When he made it home early the next morning, Natalia burst into tears. *Que hacemos ahora?* she implored the family breadwinner—what do we do now? His first attempt to start a new life had lasted all of twenty-four hours.

Back on Craigslist, he spotted jobs in hotel kitchens on Mexico's beaches, and soon was cooking for thousands of tourists at a resort in Los Cabos, though "chef" seemed too grand a title for the loathsome work of defrosting vats of frozen shrimp, chicken, and fish and frying them up for the buffet. Towers of grimy dishes sat fetid for days when the dishwashers quit. A disgusted Lalo followed them not long after.

In the U.S., where George W. Bush was already deep into his second term as a tough-on-immigration president in a post-9/11 world, Bistro VG manager Jennifer Velazquez helped organize a letter-writing campaign on Lalo's behalf: co-workers, former employers, the family dentist, loyal diners, wrote to Bush as well as to senators, asking for an exception for the model farmworker who "proved to be responsible even though he started working at a young age," the friend who "has gotten caught in the wave of political correctness," the chef who "creates dishes that tickle the palate." The pleas had no impact on his case.

Lalo's absence was felt in the restaurant. PURE was a hit; over time, it would grow to seven locations, a success built in part on Lalo's foundational work in creating the first menu. But as a deportee, Lalo wouldn't get a chance to share in that success. And he didn't hold onto hope of continuing his relationship with Max's mother—he'd been having an affair before he was deported, and he thought she'd likely moved on as well. After all, Lalo had told her there was no way he would be able to come back. But he continued talking with his son on the phone, and searching for a job so he could send them money. His first promising lead was at a boutique beach hotel called Verana. On the water taxi from Puerto Vallarta, he approached the shore of Yelapa and saw the hillside where the luxury guesthouses and private infinity pools peeked out from the thick jungle. Lalo felt his anxiety lighten for the first time in years: was it possible he'd been deported to heaven? The interview went well, but the job wouldn't start for a few weeks as the hotel was still closed for the season. Back in the Estado de México, Lalo sat in an internet cafe doing research. He Googled "best chef in Mexico," "best restaurant in Mexico."

Enrique Olvera. Pujol. Enrique Olvera. Pujol. Enrique Olvera. Pujol. It seemed almost like a glitch in the algorithm: every result was the same. Lalo thought to himself, if he gives me a job, I won't go to Verana.

On the day Lalo dialed Pujol, Olvera happened to pass by the ringing phone and pick up. Lalo ran down his résumé, and the name Eric Ripert was all it took for Olvera to invite him for an interview— it was a plate of foie gras and black truffles at Le Bernardin that had convinced Olvera he wanted to become a fine dining chef. One of Lalo's uncles owned a small fleet of microbuses and let him catch a ride the next day into the city. He stepped off in front of Chapultepec Park, twice the size of New York's Central Park, where *chilangos*, or Mexico City locals, and tourists were milling past museums and sculptures, pushing strollers through the botanical gardens, and eating corn on the cob caked with mayonnaise, cheese, lime juice, and chile. In 2007, Mexico was on edge. The presidential election of the previous year had ended with claims of illegitimacy when Andrés Manuel López Obrador lost to Felipe Calderón. Though the nation was experiencing a historic low in homicides, security was at the forefront of public discussion; Calderón began his presidency by declaring war on the country's powerful drug cartels, and tens of thousands of troops were deployed across Mexico. The battles that followed served to further disorient the nation, splinter the cartels into more aggressive factions, and lay bare not only the violence of organized crime, but the corruption that undercut the possibility of vanquishing it. Surrounded on all sides by these threats, Mexico City was considered an island of safety.

Despite having spent his early years just a few miles away, Lalo had never walked the streets of the capital. "The impression of Mexico City I had was the same one you have when you live in the States: polluted, rude people, dangerous, dirty. Everything that's bad about a city. Nothing good." But in this neighborhood, the streets were clean. It was the rainy season, and trees and flowering vines bloomed ostentatiously in every teacup of soil. In Polanco, where Olvera had opened Pujol eight years earlier, Lalo felt like he had stepped inside one of the soap operas he and Jaime used to run home to watch on their boxy TV set: people wore tailored clothes and had expensive haircuts streaked with blond highlights. On the periphery of Parque Lincoln, diners chatted at sidewalk cafés, sipping from glasses of wine and cups of espresso, on streets with names like Carlos Dickens, Aristóteles, and Julio Verne.

It turned out that Lalo had called Olvera at a fortuitous moment. Olvera was in the process of staffing the kitchen of a new restaurant for a boutique hotel called Condesa DF and he needed someone with Lalo's level of experience at the helm. Olvera told Lalo that he could start as the sous-chef at the hotel, working under Jorge Vallejo, who would later go on to be the chef-owner of the acclaimed restaurant Quintonil. When a position in Pujol opened up worthy of Lalo's experience, he would bring him over. It was an incredible offer and Lalo didn't quite believe it himself. As they said goodbye, Olvera informed Lalo that he'd have to wait a week or two to start, until after he returned from a trip to New York. Lalo nodded in agreement, but the postscript left him uneasy.

Dark clouds were rolling in, the predictable afternoon storm, and Lalo took a seat at the bar of an Argentinian restaurant as the rain began to hammer down. The bartender served him a glass of wine and they chatted amiably. On the bus ride home, he replayed the day in his mind, still unsure if he could trust the fragile optimism he felt emerging. The next day, he returned to Polanco to wander around and began to imagine how his new life might look. He had two hypothetical jobs, but no concrete tasks to perform, no money to send to his family. When he got a call from Verana telling him it was time to return to the beach, Lalo should have said "No thanks," but he hesitated. What if Olvera, this jet-setting chef, forgot his promises? Work was purpose. Purpose meant sanity. Yes, he told the owner, he'd be there. Once he arrived at the beach, he picked fruit from the trees, walked down to the dock where fishermen arrived with boats loaded with octopus, snapper, amberjack. In the evenings, he prepared meals for the owners from the day's spoils, and they marveled. Two weeks passed before Olvera called.

"I waited for you," he told Lalo. "You never showed."

"I didn't know if you were really going to hire me," Lalo said. "I don't understand why I couldn't just start the job without you. I've never lived in this country, I don't know how things work."

Olvera gave him until the next day to decide. That night, Lalo stayed up listening as the jungle chirped and croaked and the waves surged endlessly to shore. When he'd come to Mexico, he'd been at his lowest point: his father dead, his career over, his son hundreds of miles away, his future uncertain. Here in Yelapa he'd found a chance at happiness, and it frightened him to part with it. But he knew that Olvera had propped a door open for him a beat longer than courtesy required, and he'd better walk through before it slammed shut for good. He packed his bag and took the job with Olvera.

———

On the other side of that phone call was the country's most revered contemporary chef, Enrique Olvera, whose career only continued to climb. Born to a middle-class family in Mexico City, he had taken joy in experimenting with food since boyhood, never all that interested in following recipes. The kitchen intrigued him precisely because it offered the chance to experiment and play. To Olvera, a great piece of meat or plate of pasta were delicious in their simplicity, but "you've done that already." He was eager to move on and see what else he might achieve.

As a teenager, he cooked for his friends. Soon word got around, and his classmates' parents began coming to the parties, too. He traveled to the Hudson Valley to attend the famed Culinary Institute of America, then in 1999 worked at Everest, a haute French restaurant in Chicago. But after six months he returned to Mexico to pursue the dream of opening his own restaurant, supported by modest investments from his parents' friends.

It was during his years in culinary school that Olvera began to pick up on the stereotypes Americans had about his country. They believed it was filled with poverty, violence, and some nice beaches. In New York, the version of Mexican cuisine that might have provided an entry point to complicate that perception instead seemed to reinforce it: cheap enchiladas topped with fluorescent cheese, bland jars of salsa, packaged flour tortillas with a suspiciously long shelf life. A sad imitation of Tex-Mex. Even if they made it to Cancún or Puerto Vallarta, his classmates were likely to be fed tacos stuffed with imported frozen fish and served synthetic margaritas.

At the same time, Olvera was captivated by the influence of chefs like Gastón Acurio, eight years his senior. Acurio had returned to Peru after studying at Le Cordon Bleu in France and created a fine dining vision built on his country's immense wealth of ingredients and traditions. There, Andean farmers grow more than four thousand varieties of potatoes, which vary in texture from creamy to floury to waxy; their flesh can be amethyst, magenta, gold, and they emerge from the earth in the shape of a comma, a dense bunch of grapes, a fist, a spear. Acurio's first restaurant, Astrid & Gastón, opened in Lima in 1994, and soon he was able to export the concept internationally, opening restaurants from Paris to Chicago to Doha, and feeding diners who had never heard of a *causa*—a layered dish usually made with potatoes, yellow chiles, avocado, and a protein—and never ventured beyond a Russet or a Red Bliss.

Olvera watched Acurio and thought, "I want to do the same for Mexico, because if any country has gastronomic wealth, it's Mexico! I think it's incredible that there's this dynamism and leadership in other countries that have so much less to draw from than we do here."

Olvera dubbed the restaurant Pujol (pronounced poo-yol or poo-zhol), a reference to his high school nickname—a slurred pronunciation of the pork and corn soup from Guerrero called *pozole*. The food was perhaps not great at first. As Olvera put it, "I can't think of a restaurant as shitty today." But he was always a good salesman, describing the food to one interviewer as "creative, signature cuisine." They served crab cakes with a touch of cilantro, chipotle mayonnaise, and lime juice, and a filet of tuna with a black pepper crust. He took note that the public was attracted to the Mexican-inspired dishes: miso-marinated shrimp ceviche with caramelized avocado, a foie gras terrine with guava jam.

Lalo found Olvera mystifying. Lalo was a pragmatist by necessity who relied on his work ethic, his ability to outlast anyone in the kitchen and do the most grueling jobs. Olvera was a dreamer and by the time Lalo arrived, he was spending much of his time traveling and promoting the restaurant as idea. To him, the purpose of Pujol was greater than providing a tasty meal: it was a place to surprise, titillate, and finally change a diner's perspective. Lalo remembered Olvera telling the team, "What I want you to understand is that you're working in the best restaurant in the world, and your work is to cook the best food in the world."

Olvera undoubtedly played a critical role in marking Mexico City on the global foodie map. But he was preceded more than a decade earlier by chefs Mónica Patiño of La Galvia, Carmen Ortuño of Isadora, and Alicia Gironella of Los Naranjos, who were already busy reimagining the country's fine dining establishments. These chefs were profiled in a piece by *Texas Monthly* food critic Patricia Sharpe, who provided a remarkable snapshot of a quiet revolution underway—around food, but also gender and national identity. This upheaval would lead, in what now seems inevitable fashion, to a dining scene internationally acclaimed for its seamless combination of experimentation and the celebration of cultural heritage. At the time of the article, however, reimagining what might appear in the capital's upper-crust dining rooms was considered audacious, pushing against entrenched conservatism and prejudice.

To say that Mexican food was valued in casual eateries and home kitchens across the nation is a massive understatement. Food—the cultivation of ingredients, the preparation and historical lineage of dishes, and how they reflected beliefs, sparked creativity, brought together families, and ensured survival—was the cornerstone of Mexican life. And yet, while there were a handful of white-tablecloth establishments that featured Mexican food, including La Hacienda de los Morales, Fonda El Refugio, Nico's, and the San Ángel Inn, when it came to fine dining in Mexico City, French, Italian, and Spanish cuisine dominated. Sharpe's article offers a glimpse into a pivotal period for the city's cuisine, when gender dynamics in the professional kitchen were transforming, and the Eurocentric parameters of the fine dining category were being questioned.

Sharpe discusses each restaurant's strength, attributes that might as well belong to the women themselves. She dubs La Gal-via the most modern, Isadora the most poetic, and Los Naranjos the most intellectual. All three women were upper-class and media-genic, which is to say light-skinned—and they knew how to cook. It would have been one thing to simply pair previously siloed flavors and then take a bow, but the execution was exemplary. From Giro-nella, Sharpe samples ice cream flavored with mamey, a tropical fruit with a tough outer skin and orange flesh the texture of a cooked yam. She says it tastes of the "juiciest, most heavenly peach you've ever eaten," with a hint of mango, a life-changing scoop. Ortuño's ravioli stuffed with *huitlacoche** in a poblano cream sauce was a revelation.

The medium is the message, whether it was the design of Isa-dora's sleek dining room or the punch of chile that complemented a traditionally French sauce, or, in the case of these chefs, elegant professionalism from the very heart of gendered obligation: the kitchen. Gironella, Patiño, and Ortuño were questioning beliefs about Mexican identity that had been deployed since the conquest to subjugate. That subjugation had taken obvious forms: slavery, lin-guistic supremacy, a violently enforced racial hierarchy, the curtail-ing of rights and the suppression of religion. It had also manifested in gastronomy, as a defined set of norms that indicated who should cook what, what should be consumed where and with whom, per-forming class difference at every meal. This elitism ran counter to the country's supposed racial and cultural unity, a project that gained steam after the Mexican Revolution, when the newly reunited nation sought to forge a harmonious path forward after a bitter fight over economic inequality and disenfranchisement that had largely been

---

* *Huitlacoche,* also known as corn smut, is a fungus that grows on ears of corn, with a gray-blue color and a flavor redolent of mushrooms. It's often used as a filling for quesadillas and tacos.

drawn along racial lines. The figure of the mestizo, with both indigenous and European ancestry, was conceived of anew as an umbrella
identity that brought the nation together. As historian David S. Dalton writes, the insistence on *mestizaje* was ultimately an attempt to
recategorize and, in the process, transform indigenous peoples into
mestizos, coercing them to move away from a way of life considered
"backward" or "primitive" and participate in modern systems, like
industrialized agriculture and manufacturing. But even as *mestizaje*
was officially promoted, in the dining rooms of the elite the prefer-
ence for European cuisine betrayed the hierarchy that remained.

In retrospect, it seems almost too easy; there were so many
ingredients and concepts that lent themselves naturally to these mar-
riages, so many compelling flavors that simply hadn't been afforded
the institutional respect that their European counterparts had
enjoyed for centuries. Tropical fruit ice cream? Neveria Roxy had
been serving locally sourced flavors since the 1940s. Huitlacoche-
stuffed pasta? It's hard to believe a home chef wasn't inspired to make
such a natural pairing earlier. But making those seemingly innocu-
ous connections in elite spaces was a risky business proposition: the
attitudes that had for so long privileged European techniques and
flavors hadn't disappeared overnight, and a chef like Patiño couldn't
be entirely sure if an audience would follow. By the time Lalo got to
Mexico in 2007, Olvera was enjoying a surge of publicity, and his
restaurant would be on a list of the top fifty in the world for years to
come. But when Olvera first opened the doors to Pujol at the turn
of the millennium, there were days when no customers came at all.
There were no Instagram hashtags to help them make these new concepts go viral, no Michelin stars to hope for.

The women in Sharpe's profile knew what they were up to. "My
style is without borders," Patiño said. Ortuño went a step further: "I

don't consider mine a new cuisine, but a new way of seeing." These were not just establishments with good lighting and superior service. They were the hallowed rooms where negotiations were made— regarding government, business, and matrimony.

But in a deeper sense, these were not firsts. Think of women like Natalia, laboring over their own "little experiments." Sometimes they were performed in home kitchens, sometimes by street vendors who cooked up such mainstays as *tacos arabes*, a mashup of tacos and shawarma authored by Lebanese immigrants, resulting in cumin-marinated pork roasted on a spit and tucked into a thin pita. Sometimes they were undertaken in the interest of papering over internal divisions, as in the 1831 Mexican recipe book *El Cocinero Mexicano*, whose anonymous author included dishes that had already begun to blend European and indigenous foodways. As historian Sarah Bak-Geller Corona writes, the act of cataloguing these recipes homogenized the food itself, narrowing diverse ingredients, measurements, and methods into an accepted traditional version, and affirming that the elite cook who prepared said version (or instructed their employee to do so) met the emerging definition of Mexican, too.

Colonizers and their criollo and mestizo descendants had eaten plenty of indigenous food since the conquest, but the consumption of these foods came to be governed by rules of etiquette as the upper class sought to differentiate their status. Tamales could be consumed under specific circumstances, as a casual meal eaten on the sidewalk, or in the privacy of one's own home when prepared by one's cook. Over centuries, home cooks drew on imported ingredients and created novel combinations, though without the attention of critical reviews—other than from, say, picky family members. By the time Sharpe wrote her profile, the dishes that appeared in the rarefied dining rooms of Isadora and La Galvia had the sheen of something new; in reality, they were a series of riffs on centuries-old melodies.

As this culinary movement took off in the early 1990s, the city was still recovering from the catastrophic 1985 earthquake. The 8.1 temblor killed an estimated 10,000 people and laid ruin to thousands of buildings. The effects were acutely felt in the low-lying Condesa and Roma neighborhoods, the muddy foundations of which were built on the bottom of the lake that had formerly surrounded the island city of Tenochtitlan. Here, as the unstable soil vibrates, the churning movement of an earthquake can be amplified by as much as one hundred times. Many inhabitants of these formerly affluent neighborhoods decamped for stable digs to the west; within a few years, young creatives, including budding restaurateurs, were enticed by the architectural wonders and low rents left behind.

It was a chaotic decade, and no year better encapsulates that tumult than 1994, when journalist Alma Guillermoprieto wrote that the nation felt as though it were "precariously balanced on the head of a pin." A Zapatista uprising kicked off on January 1, launching a protracted fight in the southern state of Chiapas for land redistribution and better treatment of the country's indigenous peoples. Soon after, the ruling party's presidential candidate was assassinated; with that destabilizing act came the possibility that a different political party would come to power for the first time in sixty-five years. The dramatic kidnapping of Alfredo Harp Helú, one of the country's richest men, splashed across front pages until it finally ended more than one hundred days later in a $30 million ransom payment. Violence, upheaval, and uncertainty came to define both the political sphere and the personal. From the plunging value of the peso to the ratification of the North American Free Trade Agreement (NAFTA), the future of the country's workforce, their land rights, and the ability of households to put food on the table were in jeopardy.

Kidnappings became a specter in the news cycle, scaring away tourists and putting the city on high alert. A businessman warned readers of the *New York Times* of the city's ills with the dramatic flair of an older sibling at a campfire: "Everyone who comes in here has a story. Nightmarish stories, like waiting at a green light and all of a sudden three guys get into your car with guns and say, 'OK, let's go to your house.'"

Pollution was also no small detail. Mexico City acquired a worldwide reputation for a yellow-gray haze of smog that sat like rancid soup in a mountainous bowl. You can see how Lalo's picture of a sooty, crime-ridden metropolis was reinforced.

And yet, it was against this backdrop that a new style of Mexican cuisine emerged, following France's nouvelle cuisine revolution of the 1960s and 1970s, which pivoted away from heavy, traditional fare toward luxurious food that emphasized fresh ingredients in small portions. Suddenly, chefs began to think more about form, since images of their creations might be published in Mexico's fledgling food-oriented magazines and newspaper supplements. Of the rising stars from that period, Mónica Patiño is the name most likely to be familiar to locals today. Like Olvera, she was young when she opened her first restaurant—in her case, just twenty-one. It was called La Taberna del León and was located a couple of hours outside of Mexico City in Valle de Bravo, where well-to-do chilangos escaped on weekends to gulp in some literal fresh air. Customers came to visit her as much as the restaurant, charmed by this beautiful, poised young woman working to make something of her own, and brought her cookbooks from their trips abroad.

Patiño is now in her sixties, in the enviable position of having successful, enduring businesses and many accomplishments, a role model who is stopped in the street and adored and could as easily spend her days traveling the globe as tending to her restaurants. She was exposed early to her family's outside-the-box approaches to cooking and eating. In her grandmother's stately mansion in the Roma, Patiño often dined on French and Italian food, but with Mexican twists: vol-au-vent, a light, bowl-shaped pastry, was filled not with the traditional spinach, mushroom, and gruyère, but with *rajas*—strips of poblano pepper cooked in cream sauce—and spicy chorizo. At cocktail hour, her father might sip whisky or tequila, with a dish of crunchy *chicharrones*—fried pork skins—to snack on, and a bowl of Spanish olives.

"Maybe you had a cook from Oaxaca, and another from Puebla, so each one brought her way of cooking and her perspective," Patiño said of two of the country's most gastronomically prolific states. She ate Sonoran creations at her aunt's house, like pinto beans cooked in evaporated milk ("We liked the combination!"), and handmade tortillas filled with nopales, served with champagne.

"It was natural—we had that mixture in our blood. When they served dishes from the southeast, from Puebla, from Oaxaca, you understood it. But when they served French food that was well prepared, you understood it, too. It was very easy; you didn't feel any incongruence to have those cultures together at one table. Because our blood, that historical *mestizaje*, is carried inside of us, in our DNA."

Patiño's family claimed Mexican and Italian lineage, and Patiño had lived in England, Switzerland, and France by the time she opened La Taberna del Léon. As she returned to Mexico from these stints abroad, she was confounded by the experience of "living in such a rich country and perceiving it as poor." It was this dissonance that ultimately led many of the country's greatest chefs to return, like artists who felt marooned abroad with just a few pieces of charcoal at their disposal, imagining the masterpieces they might create back home in Mexico with the country's palette of cerulean blue, magenta, and chartreuse.

While Patiño had a privileged upbringing, she left high school early and set out on her own at age eighteen, renouncing her family's support. She was full of questions about the meaning of life and determined to forge her own path toward the answers.

"I always say that ignorance is what hurts you," Patiño said as she sat in the dining room of her restaurant, Casa Virginia, "but it's also what forces you to grow: when it hurts, you want to take away the pain, so you start asking, learning, practicing. Little by little, that pain starts to fade and you start having all kinds of new experiences. I started to dedicate myself to filling the emptiness I had inside."

She had her first child at age nineteen, and while she reconciled with her family, she never lived under their roof again. Her father gave her a loan to open La Taberna del León, which she paid back week by week. She modeled clothes for improvised fashion shows at the restaurant, which eventually allowed her to save enough money to return to Europe and study cooking. Later, her father would become one of the investors in her other successful restaurants.

When Patiño began to include Mexican food on her restaurant's menu, her father disapproved. He might have happily enjoyed tostadas and tacos at home, but he was an admirer of the Michelin guide, back when it only covered European countries, and came from a generation that still held fast to rigid expectations about what food could be served where and to whom. But Patiño was unimpressed by the antiquated version of French food that was commonly served in Mexico: *cuisine classique*, with its heavy sauces and identical garnishes, stuffy fare that seemed to suffer when deprived of the Mexican touches incorporated at her aunt and grandmother's tables. For food writer Alonso Ruvalcaba, one of Patiño's dishes stood out: a plate of miniature *tostadas de tinga*: shredded chicken warmed in a tomato–chile sauce on top of a crisp tortilla, topped with lettuce and *crema*, a simple, homey dish prepared all over Mexico. Patiño's La Taberna del Léon was ornately wallpapered, with stained glass windows; the waiters wore ties and a pianist played in the entryway. "Tostadas de tinga—which are totally ordinary—when put in an environment that doesn't correspond? It gives you a little shock. I loved it!" Ruvalcaba said. "Now, it seems like the most normal thing on earth. How strange that it was surprising! But it was. It was surprising. It was an intelligent thing to do."

The restaurant broke new ground, and Patiño never stopped. She was insistent on hyper-local, quality ingredients; she opened a restaurant, Naos, which combined Mexican and Asian concepts; and she began to serve an expansive list of mezcal.

In fact, she offered a mezcal cart, akin to a cart circulating cheese or dessert. A server would bring the bottles of *espadín, madre cuishe,* and *pechuga* to a dining public that had no clue what these terms denoted, and then engage in the awkward dance of trying to sell them on a beverage that most of the elite still considered to be the equivalent of moonshine. Patiño herself had grown up drinking mezcal, but only a few brands that were then available in Mexico City. While tequila is traditionally made from just one kind of maguey plant—blue agave—mezcal can be made from several dozen types, by some estimates nearly fifty. Historically produced by small-time purveyors in the villages where maguey is cultivated and harvested from the wild, with certain varieties taking decades to mature, the liquor ferments in clay or wood, cement or even leather, and sometimes a raw chicken breast, fruit, or an iguana is suspended in the steam above the still for special batches. Mezcal had not been embraced as belonging in the dining rooms of the elite, just as the upper class enjoyed tamales when eaten from a sidewalk vendor, at a festival, or with family during the holidays, but not at the table of an expensive restaurant.

Patiño began to learn about mezcal at an event in Oaxaca, and she became fascinated. She returned to rural distilleries to study further, then bought up a truckload of mezcal and brought it to Naos in Mexico City, along with an expert from Oaxaca to teach the waiters so they could pass this knowledge on to customers. They created a new menu, specifying the type of maguey, the method of distillation, the number of liters produced, the name of the master distiller who had created it, and the percentage of alcohol. Two months later, she got a call from her father who apologetically informed her that the project would have to be discontinued. Probably some bureaucratic glitch, she thought: they'd lost their license, there had been trouble with regulations. No, he told her—the waiters are anguished, they can't sell mezcal.

Patiño was furious as she called a staff meeting. "I said, 'What's going on with you *pendejos*? I'm trying to raise our mezcal to the same level as a whiskey or a cognac! What aren't you understanding?'" Heads bowed, arms crossed, they had to be prodded before Patiño discovered that she, in fact, was the one who didn't comprehend.

"Every time they approached a table with a bottle of mezcal, they felt like they were being looked at through this lens: 'the poor who wear sandals, the poor who wear cotton suits, the poor who wear sombreros and live in the sierra, the poor who drink mezcal.'" Patiño was emboldened. Why should they be made to feel that a drink indigenous to their country deserved less respect than the French wine they served? "I decided, I'm not going to end this project, my father isn't going to, either. I'm going to strengthen it! They didn't want to sell mezcal because we've been trampled upon: the colonizers— the Spanish, the French—saying that everything outside of here is greener, that the grass is greener on the other side. Which proves that we're still just servants of this ideal of development and growth, that we continue to believe that we're poor Mexicans, and that tortillas are for the poor and bread is for the rich. So, with mezcal, I decided I was going to wrap myself in the flag."

Patiño was among the first restaurateurs in Mexico City to promote what would become an international sensation, a love affair with a drink so passionate that it now lies in peril of becoming inaccessible to the people who still visit their local *palenque* to commission a special batch for a celebration, or just to get a refill. The qualities that once caused chilangos to reject the spirit—the remote locations where it is made, the enigmatic flavor and production methods—have now become part of its allure, details to geek out about when your buddy comes home from a trip with a Pepsi bottle full of a clear substance and tells you about the spot where he bought it, or bragging rights abroad for the budding connoisseur who can expound on the process of distilling a pechuga.

These dynamics are driving producers to create mezcal differently for a higher-paying, foreign customer base that has gravitated toward single-maguey distillations, eschewing the practice of combining various types of maguey into a single batch. For a prized wild varietal like *tepeztate*, online reviewers detect bubblegum, poblano peppers, cacao nibs, asparagus, vanilla, cinnamon, guava, unripe avocados, banana, ginger, broccolini, cucumber peel, peat, watermelon rind, with a "wet hay note that I wish I could make a candle of," and "maybe some lilac soap? followed by some gentle ash—like from a dead campfire that burned out overnight, not the one you just dumped water on—as well as some warm cedar wood, maybe some rose water." It's easy to forget that ten years before typing up their reviews, it's unlikely that these aficionados would have sampled any mezcal, that Patiño rushed to her restaurant to find a mutiny of waiters refusing to sell a drink that provoked widespread condescension in its birthplace.

Mexican is hardly a monolithic identity. More than sixty indigenous languages are spoken across the country. In the sixteenth and seventeenth centuries, the region became a significant recipient of enslaved Africans. *Conversos*, or Jews who converted to Catholicism amid violent anti-Semitism, arrived there after fleeing the Spanish Inquisition, and Lebanese, Syrian, Iraqi, Colombian, Caribbean, Chinese, and Central American communities have shaped local culture, not to mention the North African influences brought by Spanish colonists. City kids like Patiño and Olvera have traveled extensively, sampling distinct techniques and ingredients to get to know each region of their country. Patiño recalled a trip she'd taken as a teenager, into a town in the mountains of Oaxaca called Huautla. Her cadence quickened as she described the ten-hour drive on the highway, waking up at dawn surrounded by a blanket of fog. She saw a pillar of smoke rising from a nearby house and approached, smelling firewood. A woman was making tortillas by hand and there was a pot of simmering beans. The woman prepared salsa in a *molcajete*, a mortar and pestle made of volcanic rock. It was the best meal she'd had in her life. When Olvera speaks in interviews, he often talks about a day when he ate *hormigas chicatanas*, the delicacy of large, brown flying ants available fresh during just a handful of days each year when their nests flood with the first spring rainstorms. Tasting those ants was one of the emotional high points of his life, he says, on par with the opening day of Pujol.

Lalo came from one of those rural towns that his mentors might have visited in search of inspiration, towns where cooking techniques had evolved over millennia. Some innovations were the happy result of a wealth of ingredients. Others, like the consumption of ants, are likely owed to conditions of scarcity. When Lalo arrived in Olvera's kitchen in 2007, the experiments they were performing with food looked not unlike a scientific laboratory. Olvera took inspiration from the cuisine of Mexico, and cues from restaurants like Alinea and El Bulli to make gels, foams, and flavor orbs that bore little resemblance to their origins. Molecular gastronomy had reached its experimental heights in the hills of Catalonia. Anytime a chef returned to Mexico having staged there, they earned respect and admiration.

Olvera and Lalo fell into a pattern. Lalo listened skeptically as Olvera tried to convince him of the merits of experimentation, even when the results didn't taste as good as the classics. To his fellow cooks, Lalo's pedigree was also suspect. They called him a *pocho*, slang for someone who has left Mexico to live in the U.S. and returned. You might call a buddy a pocho affectionately, but usually the word carries derogatory connotations, implying that the returnee is ignorant of his birth country and has come back with a condescending attitude toward both Mexico and his countrymen. Literally, *pocho* translates to faded or wilted. But, like Olvera, his colleagues in the kitchen watched Lalo micromanaging every detail, never too proud to complete a menial task if it might improve their collective work.

Lalo was confounded by the amount of time Olvera spent on the road, but his traveling paid off. Tourists began to visit and word spread. "Mexico was a folkloric place for the world. Now it's seen as much more sophisticated, without losing that sense of joy that people associate with Mexico," Olvera said. People came to visit for the country's trademark hospitality, "and we *are* hospitable and we *do* know how to throw a party, but I also think people knew Mexico from an outsider's perspective, from the bubble of a hotel property." Pujol became a gateway restaurant for gourmands—the destination that drew them in, before they discovered how much more awaited them.

Olvera wasn't the first dreamer Lalo had worked for; Ripert and the Sedgwicks also aspired to reach ever greater heights with their restaurants. Lalo had spent years as the head of his own kitchen, but he was ready and willing to serve Olvera's vision. Returning from a trip inspired, Olvera would walk into the kitchen and tell his cooks to make a liquid quesadilla. Lalo would stand back and observe as his colleagues gamely tested recipes until they'd created a spoonful that pleased Olvera. Then, Lalo would make sure that every liquid quesadilla—a brew of cheese and *comal**-toasted masa served like a shot of tequila—made it to the customer exactly as Olvera had ordained.

Olvera continued to push beyond convention by bringing street food into the dining room. In *Veinte*, a book chronicling Pujol's first two decades, Alonso Ruvalcaba writes that "restaurants wanted nothing to do with street food, and street food did not aspire to the supposed elevation of restaurants," before the twenty-first century. At Pujol, tacos began to show up on the menu, but they were inevitably reimagined until they were barely recognizable. A taco was layered in a jar like a trifle. Tortillas were reinterpreted as air or powder. In time, those funhouse mirror transformations faded. Ruvalcaba writes of sea bass accompanied by pineapple, green chile, lime, and cilantro—typical toppings for *tacos al pastor*. "The dish was crying

---

* A *comal* is a flat cooking surface—a griddle—and one of the foundational tools of the Mexican kitchen. A comal can be made of various materials, including cast iron, untreated clay, steel, and volcanic rock.

out, 'Let me be a taco.'" Soon enough, Olvera seemed to hear its call. "And then, as inevitable as the earth rotating, the sea bass became a bonafide taco. One that was wrapped in a corn tortilla; one which you poured salsa on and grabbed with your hand; one which you held whole with your fingers and took to your mouth more or less diagonally. *Well, a taco.*"

Over the next decade, Pujol would begin to embrace the taco in its classic form. Tortillas became a critical feature of the menu and in the life of the kitchen. The restaurant reopened in 2017 in a building especially conceived to pair with Olvera's vision. The space is warm yet restrained, featuring hardwood furniture and ceilings, and terrazzo floors. The large windows at the back frame an exuberant green garden, gobbling up the abundant sunlight. The kitchen is as remarkable as the dining room: oriented around Mexican techniques, the stations include a wood-fired grill and a prominent comal where a cook is positioned throughout service, making tortillas; outside, there's a *barbacoa* pit and native herbs growing in the garden. It was also in 2017 that Olvera made an attention-grabbing announcement: the new Pujol would feature an *omekase* taco menu. *Omekase* is the Japanese term for a chef's choice and is typically applied to sushi. At Pujol, diners embark on a lengthy meal composed of tacos and snacks that changes with the seasons.

Today, Olvera is no longer chasing a surrealist fantasy. He wants diners at Pujol to experience a meal of exceptional flavor, which holds itself to a high standard, sourced from the country's best seafood, produce, insects, dairy, and meat. A meal that celebrates Mexico as it was, and as it might be tomorrow—infused with new ideas from young chefs that complement rather than control what ultimately makes it onto the plate. Olvera pays homage to his country's bounty, but he doesn't feel obliged to loyally follow "authentic" recipes or techniques. He's still the kid in the kitchen who'd rather play than follow the steps in someone else's cookbook.

One of the restaurant's iconic dishes survived the transition from the first Pujol to today's custom dining room: young ears of corn slathered with chicatana ant and chile mayonnaise. The dish arrives at the table in a hollow gourd. When the top is removed, a plume of smoky condensation escapes, leaping toward you. It recalls the street snack of corn slathered in mayonnaise, crumbly cotija cheese, lime juice, and chile—except this corn, speared with a toothpick, can be eaten whole, and rests on a bed of charred cornhusks.

In time, Lalo would appreciate the fruits of Olvera's labor away from the kitchen. It was a different kind of work, a process of education and hard-earned publicity that made Olvera a sort of patron saint for the city's other restaurateurs, augmenting tourism and therefore the money that flowed in. After working for him, cooks would depart and open their own restaurants, confident that many of the guests who came to dine at Pujol would find them, too. Just as Patiño had become a new voice in a centuries-long dialogue, Olvera added his own perspective.

As much as Lalo came to admire Olvera and the value of his mission, he couldn't imagine stepping back from the day-to-day.

"I wouldn't miss it for the world to cook for you, to be the one to cut the fish, to be the one who made the sauce. I wouldn't miss it for the world! Why would I miss that to be somewhere else?"

CHAPTER SEVEN

MÁXIMO BISTROT LOCAL

IN THE FALL of 2011, Lalo stood in a muddy ditch in the middle of a former wheelchair shop. The cost of having a cistern profession-ally installed in his new restaurant was $3,000. Instead, Lalo bought a heavy hammer, whacked through the tile floor and began to dig. Underneath he found black mud—the bottom of the lake that once surrounded the island city of Tenochtitlan—and an empty casket. It took three days for Lalo to dig out the 5,000-liter cistern that would hold the restaurant's water. Years later, friends and relatives would keep this image of Lalo in their minds: muddy, possessed, in motion, sculpting his restaurant by hand.

Except, it was not only his. A few years earlier, Lalo had met Gabriela López Cruz, then the food and beverage manager of the Condesa DF hotel. They were opposites in many ways, the kind that attract. She, a petite yogini with a joyous laugh that sent her body pitching conspiratorially forward. She, who had grown up with finan-cial stability, a diploma in restaurant management, stylish clothes, a good haircut, an even temperament. Lalo, broad-shouldered and unkempt, whose daily workout involved carrying heavy pots and darting around the kitchen. Lalo, who could be disconcertingly distant, or intoxicatingly passionate. Gaby's parents doted on her, never uttered an insult, and, as members of Mexico's small middle class, they had used all of their resources to put their three daughters through a private school barely within their means. Lalo and his parents rarely embraced and never proclaimed their "I love you"s explicitly; Lupe had doled out discipline with his hand, and Natalia with curses, but their love was evident from acts of service: Lalo's risky journey back from Mexico to care for Lupe as he died of cancer, and the bowl of pozole Natalia made for him when he arrived.

It was Gaby who noticed Lalo first. To her, he looked like a dark-featured Leonardo DiCaprio: intense eyes, a wide face, and arched brows that made his gaze almost feline. Gaby, a vegetarian, was accustomed to making do by eating quesadillas with beans and nopales on a daily basis, but when Lalo saw that she was excluded from the meat-based staff meals, he began to cook for her. This special consideration must be a sign of interest, she thought.

Why don't we go get a coffee, she asked Lalo. How about a drink sometime? No, he was busy, always busy. If he wasn't working, he was commuting an hour or two back to the family house in the Estado de México, where he still lived.

Gaby had dreamed about a career as a restaurateur since she was a little girl. Instead of toys or clothes, she always asked to eat at a fancy restaurant as her birthday gift. One year it might be Mónica Patiño's La Taberna del Léon, another El Lago, the grand dining room that overlooked a lake in Chapultepec Park. She attended a master's program in hospitality and later saved up to study yoga in India. Though Gaby was every bit the pragmatic boss, she made her most important decisions based on intuition. In Lalo, she sensed the presence of a good soul, battered by a series of trials. She was drawn to him and accepted as facts what others might have perceived as red flags.

The couple had more in common than it may seem: both were obsessed with the pursuit of perfection in their work and used their rare pockets of free time to enjoy fine meals and good wine. They were ravenous to explore what could be done in the restaurant space, and quick to discard trends that read more like gimmicks in favor of quality hospitality, excellent cooking, and intimate spaces. Gaby was interested in aesthetics, to be sure: she loved good perfume and adapted her own version of British-schoolgirl style from model Alexandra Chung, favoring miniskirts with knee socks and leather brogues. But, like Lalo, her family was at the center of her life, and she valued relationships and experiences more than the things money could buy.

One night, Lalo had to close the kitchen and open it again early the next morning. The journey to and from the house in the Estado would take up most of those hours and only add to his exhaustion.

"Can you find me a hotel room to stay in?" he asked Gaby.

"You can sleep in my apartment if you want," she told him. It was just a few blocks away. She'd given up on hoping the offer would result in something other than sleep, but when she came home from her shift, he woke up and they finally had that drink.

"Well, one thing led to another," she said.

They spent their free days eating and drinking around Mexico City, tasting everything on offer. By and large, the city's fine dining restaurants weren't all that great, they decided. The decent ones had a stuffy formality that belonged to a different generation. If you wanted to eat well, you were usually better off finding a great taco stand on the sidewalk, a long line signifying that something extraordinary awaited inside the cart. Gaby's unapologetic critiques of the restaurant scene were thrilling to Lalo, who believed indifference to be among the worst—and most common—vices in his fellow man. Together, they could dissect for hours the flaws of a dish or the service in the restaurants they visited, and relished imagining how they could do it better, together. Their dream was simple: a restaurant of their own, focused on food. Gaby at the front of the house, Lalo in the kitchen.

Lalo had long since stopped hearing from Max's mother. He could understand why: he'd cheated on her and grown distant and apathetic, even as she cared for him and Max. The fact that he later felt repentant couldn't make up for those past mistakes. His early union with Gaby wasn't idyllic either. There was infidelity and lying on both sides. Gaby sometimes felt like Lalo was speaking in a different language. An offhand comment would haunt her for days. One day, the toilet clogged and Gaby asked him for help. Lalo unclogged it easily, then said, "*Me queda claro que para pendejo no se estudia.*" Clearly, some people are born idiots. Gaby grabbed her keys and the dog and set out for a walk before he could see the tears streaming down her cheeks.

"I couldn't believe that a guy would treat me this way. In my house growing up, my father always treated us like queens, like ladies. Suddenly I'm with this guy I'm in love with and he starts saying these words. To me!"

They argued and reconciled. Went to a therapist. Stopped seeing other people. Made a pledge to tell the truth. They argued and reconciled. The arguments tended to be less explosive and the happy periods between them longer.

Regardless of the day's romantic temperature, they always had work in common. Gaby was in awe of Lalo's cooking and his work ethic. Lalo respected Gaby's excellence as a manager; she drew his attention to the evasive qualities that make a restaurant excel, beyond the food. They began to fill in an imaginary restaurant with ever greater detail, and decided to leave Olvera's businesses to spend a season working at the beach hotel Verana to plan. Lalo was welcomed back, along with Gaby as the restaurant's host and only waitress. During the nine-month season, they lived in a small house made of concrete block with a thatched roof. There was a mountain stream running past and a stand of mango trees. After work, Lalo would take their black lab, Otto, into the jungle and go fishing, usually without much success, then build a fire and cook for Gaby as they watched dolphins jump over the horizon line.

At Verana, many of the stressors—and many of their problems— seemed to disappear. They made aguas frescas with the passion fruit they picked from the trees, and ceviche from freshly caught fish. Gaby considered their time at the hotel a mini-training, a test of how they'd work together once they opened their own restaurant. The hotel had a small, loyal customer base—mostly foreigners looking for the privacy afforded by the individual casitas and remote location. Among them were a few celebrities, an Argentinian printing magnate, and an interior designer from San Francisco named Charles de Lisle.

————

The recession was hitting hard when de Lisle saw a travel deal pop-up in his inbox. Though he couldn't exactly afford a vacation, he thought to himself, I have to get out of here.

De Lisle approached the steep hillside by boat. When it docked, a porter strapped his bag to a mule and together they began to climb. In the hotel library, he greedily assembled a stack of books on Mexican architecture, then sat next to the pool absorbed in their pages.

De Lisle had never considered himself a foodie like his friends in Northern California, who obsessed over chefs and reviews the way some people keep tabs on fantasy football. But when he was served lunch, "it was simple and elegant and amazing and perfect. I thought, 'This is incredible. What's up with that?'"

"Oh," Gaby told him, "the cook is my boyfriend. His name is Lalo." De Lisle took in the cooking setup: a single propane burner, a five-gallon jug of water, a bucket, a knife. After a few days of eating Lalo's food, chatting with Gaby, and lounging by the pool, de Lisle joined them for a day trip into the mountains in search of regional fare. They didn't find much besides an ancient bakery and a decent taco stand, but they ended up becoming friends. "I instinctively fell in love with them both, right away."

De Lisle noticed the way Lalo ate. Wherever they went, he would order virtually everything on the menu, then go about investigating the components with his hands. He'd pick up a taco, but he'd also squeeze the stewed meat between his fingers, or plunge his thumb into a piece of fruit.

"He'll get in this zone. He could be talking about whatever, and he's digging in with his hands, moving from one plate to another like he's a little kid."

Lalo and Gaby noticed the way de Lisle examined the details of Mexican design: haciendas decorated with plaster reliefs of seashells, religious iconography that radiated uncommon warmth, a narrative of place and family thriving in the presence of a beneficent God. De Lisle could link an aesthetic with a feeling, a motif, a historical reference, through the medium of his own playful spirit.

A few months later, Lalo and Gaby called de Lisle to tell him that they were getting ready to open their own restaurant, and they wanted him to be the designer. Why me, he wondered, of all people?

Well, they said, we want it to feel familiar and distinctive at the same time—as comfortable as a family home in Mexico, but with the subtle sophistication of a French bistro. When they looked at Mexico City restaurants, they seemed to be either traditional or imitations of modernist concepts that had been popularized in other Latin American cities. Then they'd remembered de Lisle, who had arrived at the beach and promptly stuck his head in a stack of books about Mexican architecture. Maybe, in coming from the outside, he could reinterpret familiar influences in a new way.

De Lisle told them he'd do the job for free if they showed him around Mexico City. For the next year, they flew him down and ate everywhere together: loncherias, taquerias, upscale Italian restaurants, and what they deemed horrible French restaurants. De Lisle would crash at their place or stay in a seedy hotel. Lalo and Gaby kept funding his plane tickets but had stopped paying their electricity bill.

Before de Lisle met the couple, the recession had forced him to downsize from a staff of twelve to just one, from managing twenty-five projects to just one. But the crisis also catalyzed a moment of clarity: he had nothing to lose. Now, he'd gained two new friends in a foreign city, and was in the midst of creating something he was truly proud of. De Lisle took in the cantinas and colonial mansions, the taquerias and living rooms, the use of light in the modernist designs of Mexican architect Luis Barragán. The location they had found, on a quiet corner in the Roma, was a wheelchair supply shop on the first floor of a small three-story residential building. De Lisle reimagined the space as an intimate bistro composed of three white rooms joined by open archways, with bright green tiled floors, green plaid curtains woven by Oaxacan artisans, black Lightolier fixtures from the 1950s, and dark wood tables, chairs, and benches carved from a single, massive mesquite tree.

The overall effect was unfussy and intimate; it didn't call attention to itself. Naturalistic touches could be found throughout: cinnamon-brown ceramic pitchers overflowing with fresh flowers, a chandelier above the bar where birds swooped through metal leaves, and the focal point of the restaurant: the tree of life. Inspired, in part, by the religious iconography de Lisle had seen in eighteenth-century haciendas on their road trip, they sculpted a raised plaster tree on the wall closest to the entrance. Gaby found a mom-and-pop operation that repaired church reliefs, and the owner's son agreed to take on the job. De Lisle, who had earned a degree in ceramics before becoming a designer, made his own modifications to the sculpture. After it was painted white, the tree seemed to melt into the backdrop, but in the evening they put candles on its branches and set it aglow.

In those early days, before they had money, it seemed like everyone wanted to pitch in to help the young couple with stars in their eyes. An architect who had worked with Olvera offered to make the blueprints and take his payment later (they affectionately nicknamed him Arqui, for *arquitecto*), and Lalo performed whatever hard labor he could to save money, like digging the cistern on his own. It would cost thousands to paint the walls, so Lalo and Gaby hired a company to teach them the technique, then did it themselves.

When it came time to decide on a name, the only one Lalo was drawn to commemorated what he had left behind, what was missing: his son, Max. They would call the restaurant Máximo Bistrot. Gaby understood the significance, but worried it would sound arrogant. In Spanish, *máximo* means "the best." Máximo Bistrot translates literally to "the best bistro." The seeming declaration made Gaby cringe at first, but nothing else felt right. De Lisle wrote the restaurant's logo, Máximo Bistrot Local, in his own hand.

Selecting the name meant putting Lalo's son, by then eight years old, on the banner. It meant saying his son's name dozens of times a day, even when the other party in the conversation had no clue that the name had a double meaning. Lalo had not been a model father—or partner. Still, after he was deported, he believed he would continue to be in his son's life.

"For the first few months, we talked every day. I called every day—no problems. Then, one day, the phone changed. I thought, 'It's OK, there's nothing wrong.' Then the email changed. And then I called her mom and she answered and she said, 'She doesn't live here anymore.' I said, 'Do you know what happened?' She said, 'I have no idea.' I called again, the number changed. Everything changed. My mom would go sometimes to the house and beg, and her mother would say, 'I don't know anything, I don't know what happened.' My sister would go, my brother would go. They'd always say, 'I don't know what happened, not my problem.' And that's how it went."

Once, Lalo's sister Maria saw Max and his mother at the mall. She observed them from afar and slowly made her way closer until she greeted them. "What's going on?" she asked. "Where have you been?" But she couldn't get answers.

Natalia had suffered loss before: Lalo's deportation, Lupe's untimely death, her own misdiagnosis. In each case, time had slowly paved a path to acceptance. But the sudden, inexplicable loss of her relationship with her grandson ate away at her and never seemed to fade. There were framed portraits of him all around her bedroom: Max with a bowl cut grinning as he sat on top of a fire truck, Max wearing a cowboy hat in front of a faux background of the desert at sunset, Max smiling in a full Santa suit. In photo albums, there was Max curled up next to an emaciated Lupe on the couch, by then nearing the end of his battle with cancer. Lupe's face was gaunt, but you could tell he was trying to muster a smile.

Lalo imagined that maybe, one day, the boy would come looking for him. Later, Lalo would speak with lawyers and learn that the
process for arguing for legal access to his son could drag on for years
in international court, so long that Max would likely be an adult
before any agreement was reached. While he didn't consciously put
the name Máximo on the awning for that reason, it might serve as a
flare in the darkness that would guide Max back, or at least let him
know that he was missed.

————

On opening day, November 30, 2011, Máximo Bistrot had six
employees: Lalo and Gaby, two cooks, and two servers they had
met while working at Pujol. Brothers Oscar and Rubén Luna Rivera
were the waiters–hosts–bartenders; they were both from the same
remote village of Acatepec, Puebla (pop. 411), near Oaxaca, and had
come to Mexico City in search of work. They began at a restaurant
in the Zona Rosa and later moved to Pujol in Polanco. Oscar was
enamored with the daily act of learning he experienced at Pujol, and
the possibility of staying in Mexico while making a wage competitive with waiters in the U.S. Eventually, the brothers would bring
other relatives and friends from Acatepec to Mexico City to work
for Lalo. Oscar would tell them, "You don't have to go to another
country to change your story."

Gabriel (whom Lalo called Pedrito, for his alleged resemblance
to famed ranchero singer Pedro Fernández), the sous-chef, was nineteen years old, slight, smart, and good-natured. He first met Lalo at
Pujol. At the time, he was still finishing a certificate in gastronomy,
and quickly climbed the ranks from his first job as a dishwasher.
Mario, twenty-four years old, hailed from Veracruz, and split his

time between cooking and returning home for the hard but more lucrative jobs in the oil fields. The cooks took turns washing dishes.

In late November, Gaby received the call: they were finally allowed to open their doors after months in regulatory limbo, waiting for their permits to come through. That week, her neighbor Mónica wanted to throw a party to celebrate her university diploma and the event seemed to Gaby like a good way to dive in. The group of twenty was their first reservation. Guests sat along an L-shaped table and ate grilled octopus and short ribs braised in red wine, served on mismatched platters that Gaby had bought at the Lagunilla flea market. Máximo Bistrot brought in 40,000 pesos, then around $3,000, on its first day. Not bad.

The next day was a wake-up call. There were perhaps two tables, 4,000 pesos—or $300—in sales. Gaby felt like cold water had been dumped on her head.

Rubén and Oscar stood on street corners in the Roma handing out copies of the menu, which offered a prix fixe lunch: an appetizer, entrée, and desert for 130 pesos, about $10. The restaurant remained deserted. It had only been a couple of weeks, but Lalo began to panic. He told Gaby they should change course: turn it into a taqueria, at least get back the investment they'd borrowed from family. Then a minor earthquake struck, strong enough to cause the ground to sway. They stood in the street and Lalo prayed for the building to fall so they wouldn't have to face their failure.

The following week, Gaby's younger sister arranged an early Christmas party for her coworkers. Lalo and Gaby filled the dining room with candles and plants, and placed the tables next to the romantically lit windows, staging an image of the restaurant they wanted to be. Somehow, this vision began to manifest. Night after night the dining room's dark mesquite tables, once forlorn, began to fill with customers, food, laughter, celebration. Within weeks, they were turning people away from the door of the crowded restaurant, and then taking reservations weeks in advance.

In the very beginning, Lalo cooked rustic French and Italian cuisine, with few signs of Mexican influence. The menu was written out on blank paper in blocks of text, then cut out and glued to a photo of de Lisle's tree of life. When they made photocopies, it resembled a DIY flyer for a punk concert. They served standard bistro fare: steak frites, vegetable lasagna, arugula salad, steamed mussels. Over time, dishes from those early menus would be tweaked, the flavors would grow more layered and the style of plating more distinct. A dish that began as a standard would come to feel as if it had been signed by Lalo's hand. Take the roasted beet salad. He had first served it at Bistro VG, in one of his attempts to imitate a more established chef's menu. In the first months of Máximo, he prepared roasted beets with sheep milk feta cheese and a sprinkling of pomegranate seeds. Delicious, simple, pretty. Later, he would switch out the feta for yogurt sauce and add black flecks of vanilla bean. The dish began to resemble a composition by Alexander Calder: imperfect geometric shapes overlapping, each emphasizing the color and form of the next. Still later, the salad would include roasted pears, and the sweetly astringent pomegranate seeds would be reinterpreted as a pomegranate vinaigrette, a splash of acidity that harmonized with the pears and beets and the briny cheese.

Mushrooms were one of Lalo's fixations, evident in an early gnocchi dish. He enriched their earthiness with all varieties of fat: he'd sauté them in butter or olive oil, drizzle them with veal demiglace, stuff them with sweetbreads or cheese. Locally foraged wild mushrooms, thanks to Mexico's lengthy rainy season, became a mainstay on the menu. Through their reinterpretation, it was possible to observe the maturation of Lalo's culinary point of view. He possessed a relentless curiosity about where he could take his favorite ingredients, but that tinkering took place in harmony with tradition. The flavors he elicited were intense, his plating spontaneous yet disciplined. Porcini mushroom soup was pureed to peak lusciousness, then left alone to shine in its simplicity. At other times, he'd play a bit: morels were stuffed with chicken liver, porcini, and parmesan cheese, and topped with caviar. Sometimes, seared mushrooms would accompany a chicken thigh or an aged ribeye, umami unabashedly layered on umami. The technique behind those dishes was what made diners stop mid-chew. They'd murmur and groan and feed each other across the table. It was borderline inappropriate. The level of Lalo's skill was evident in the demi-glace, which was prepared in a massive pot that took up much of the kitchen's small second floor, next to the walk-in fridge. It was in the funky-deep flavor of beef, which Lalo dry-aged himself, and the careful selection of Italian truffles that would be shaved over a wild mushroom risotto, releasing their musky perfume with each bite.

And then, something else happened. Lalo began to put Mexico on the menu. He'd done it at Verana all the time: a chile, a sauce, a preparation that came from the country he had spent so many years recalling at Natalia's table, and had discovered anew with a chef's eye. Diners clamored for more. Octopus was sliced thin and served with a riot of acid and heat in an *aguachile.** A midnight-blue corn tostada was caked with sea urchin, then layered with circles of purple

---

* An *aguachile* is a spicy form of ceviche which originated in Sinaloa and incorporates raw seafood, typically shrimp or fish, lime and fresh chiles, and is served immediately rather than being allowed to marinate.

daikon radish, dots of green pureed avocado, red salsa *tatemada*,* and cilantro flowers. Red snapper was seared in olive oil and topped with an herbaceous, nutty green mole sauce, built from pumpkin seeds, sunflower seeds, cumin seeds, peppercorns, cloves, parsley, epazote, serrano pepper, tomatillos, leeks, garlic, onion, and coriander seeds.

Olvera visited the new restaurant. Having worked with Lalo for more than three years, he expected he might see some of Pujol reflected on Lalo's plate. There were a few commonalities, but the food was distinct from his own, a reflection of Lalo's obsessions.

The other thing Olvera noticed was Gaby. It was Gaby who had identified de Lisle as the right designer, Gaby who set the welcoming tone, selected the flowers and the candles and the scent of the soap in the bathroom. Indeed, it was hard to imagine what a restaurant by Lalo would have looked like without her, so central was she to every decision outside of the kitchen. "A fundamental part of the success of Máximo is Gaby. She's the opposite of Lalo, and she's what makes everything work," Olvera said. Gaby was the co-protagonist, carefully curating the restaurant experience even as Lalo, the star chef, became the name the media remembered.

Before service each day, Lalo would call the wait staff to the pass and serve them the newest additions to the menu. A dozen forks were passed around as Lalo talked about the dish and how to describe it to customers. Sometimes he'd describe a French technique or the reason a particular variety of caviar was prized. But often, the most captivating flavors on the menu came from rural Mexico, principally the state of Oaxaca. In Oaxaca alone, more than a dozen indigenous languages and dialects are spoken, and eight regions each claim a dis-

---

* Salsa *tatemada* is prepared by charring vegetables (tomatoes, chiles, garlic, and onion) directly on a hot comal, then pounding them together in a molcajete. In many households today, it's prepared in a blender. Add a little salt and it's done.

tinct cultural and culinary identity. Like Olvera, who came to regard Oaxaca as a second home, Lalo began to draw inspiration from the land of mole, mezcal, cacao, and corn.

Olvera first tasted chicatana ants when visiting Oaxacan chef Alejandro Ruiz Olmedo. Many of the techniques that would become emblematic of fine dining in Mexico City were daily pleasures in Ruiz's childhood. "It was normal to have a freshly made tortilla, it was normal to take the chiles from the plant and roast them and make a molcajete sauce," Ruiz recalled. "It was also normal to approach a lemon or orange tree and cut the oranges and lemons and prepare *limonada fresca*." In Oaxaca, food is more than sustenance— it's political. "We use food to talk about our traditions, our culture. Everywhere we go we bring ingredients." Maintaining that culture is an act of resistance, one which has successfully survived centuries of attempts at domination and diminishment.

The region's intensely local ingredients, traditional methods, and flair for innovation made Oaxaca a must-visit destination for Lalo, who was trying to get to know his country through the eyes of a chef. When they were still working for Olvera, Lalo and Gaby would board a bus at midnight and arrive in the city of Oaxaca in time for breakfast on their day off. They'd eat, drink, eat, drink, walk through the markets studying ingredients and talking with vendors, then board the last bus home with their spoils. They'd wake up at the end of the ride and head to work.

When they opened Máximo Bistrot, there was no time for such trips. And no money, even for bus fare. The gas bill unpaid, they had no hot water at home, so when the restaurant closed at 1 a.m., Lalo took an improvised shower using the hose from the dishwashing sink, then slept in the car or on the bathroom floor while he waited for Gaby to finish the accounting. There was no time to take their beloved dog Otto for walks, and he drove the apartment building crazy with his whining. One day, a neighbor called Gaby, threatening to report her for animal cruelty. Gaby broke down crying. "We can't live like this!" she told Lalo.

After service ended each evening and Gaby peeled Lalo off the bathroom floor, they'd return home, crash into bed, and then Lalo would get back up at 4 a.m. to drive to the Central de Abasto. The city's behemoth mother market—with its own toll plazas, police force, and zip code—stays open 365 days a year, and supplies everyone from restaurants to sidewalk fruit stands. When Lalo discovered Mexico City as an adult, the market became one of his favorite places. It could be overwhelming: a newcomer would have little way of navigating toward the sections required by a grocery list without a knowledgeable guide of the square-mile market. But with some direction, you could wander through piles of artichokes, stacks of laurel branches, and bouquets of yellow squash blossoms, contemplating them like works of art.

Lalo would buy a *café de olla*, sweetened with *piloncillo* (a form of unrefined sugar made by boiling sugar cane juice) and cinnamon, then walk at a clip through the aisles, grabbing the best avocados (the ones with deceptively lackluster skin), boxes of edible violas, and bags of wild morels for that day's service. The trips were partly a source of inspiration, but mainly he took on the task himself because it was cheaper than paying a middleman.

Like Olvera, Lalo watched diners gravitate toward his Mexican flavors. By the year's end, Lalo's culinary point of view was loud and clear: short ribs cooked with mole, octopus in a guajillo chile emulsion, aguachile of scallop and chocolate clams. Ingredient-centric food that confidently brought together Mexican and French concepts.

Lalo still counted Michele Sedgwick as his biggest influence, and in interviews he took care to explain the importance of local, quality ingredients on his menu. But, in other ways, he still seemed to be getting his bearings as a representative of a burgeoning culinary movement, unclear how much he wanted to reveal about his life to the media that came calling. Sometimes, he offered up white lies; they just made it a little easier to briefly frame his odyssey for a stranger. He told reporters that he had worked at the internationally acclaimed Le Bernardin, considered by many the best restaurant in the United States, even the world. He had never worked at Le Bernardin. He had indeed worked for the restaurant's head chef, Eric Ripert, but he had done so at Brasserie Le Coze. Brasserie Le Coze closed its doors in 2006 and wasn't widely known. When Lalo was a teenager, the offer had been on the table—Ripert invited him to travel to New York to work at Le Bernardin. This hypothetical trip became a highly-detailed fantasy in Lalo's mind, a *telenovela* that starred a scrawny boy from the countryside who travels to the big city to work at one of the most acclaimed restaurants in the world. It never happened, but Lalo came to offhandedly add this to his résumé. Once he'd name-dropped Le Bernardin a few times and watched the spark of recognition flare in the listener's eyes, it was impossible to take the embellishment back: Le Bernardin would be included in Lalo's biography in everything from blog posts to news coverage. Sometimes, Lalo offered dates and ages for the milestones of his childhood, unsure which ones were correct. Sometimes he compressed events that had happened across time, and then felt like he'd lost the years in between, worthless expanses that sat between more dramatic milestones.

In those first interviews after Máximo opened, Lalo was often asked to explain how he conceived of the dishes on the menu. Well, simple: he took his French training and his native cuisine, then looked at what was on offer at the Central de Abasto, and cooked. Voilà. Lalo had plenty of stories to tell about those dishes and their origins, but he chafed against the expectation of some pat anecdote. When he was asked to cook one of his favorite recipes for a TV interview or name a dish he felt proud of, he'd turn to a ribeye or asparagus with hollandaise sauce—plates of food that he simply loved, but which offered little insight into his point of view.

———

Narratives about food are usually implicit: a feast commemorating a marriage; a genocidal origin story recast with pumpkin pie, turkey, and cranberry sauce; religious traditions that encourage us to feast on noodles, eggs, pomegranates, wine, and dates. Food helps us to divine narratives of class, belief, and politics, to see the ingenuity of ancestors who turned scarcity into delicious invention. But the self-conscious role of chef as head storyteller, the role that the public increasingly wanted Lalo to inhabit, is a more recent invention, fathered to a great extent by television's eager packaging of charismatic cooks, valued as much for their ability to captivate viewers as for their cooking know-how.

"It is a problem for people who are not naturally charming," said Ruth Reichl, the food critic and author. "A lot of people who go into the kitchen do so because they're not comfortable in front of the public." When Lalo opened Máximo Bistrot, in addition to making the menu and budgetary decisions, managing the staff, and teaching less experienced cooks to master new skills, he was tasked with being the head storyteller (a.k.a. marketer). He had to make people care about the experience of eating his food, and that meant describing where it came from, what made his style of cooking distinctive, and how it recalled the past. He had witnessed the power that Olvera's project derived from his willingness and dexterity as a storyteller; narrating the restaurant's place in the culture was integral to the process of actualizing his vision.

Before Patiño or Olvera or Lalo came on the scene, Chepina Peralta and Yuri de Gortari Krauss were go-to figures for Mexican food media. Peralta was the first woman to host a cooking show in Latin America, beginning in 1967. "I understood that there were a lot of women like me who cooked for their families because they had to, but they didn't take pleasure in it," she told *Animal Gourmet.* Peralta highlighted accessible recipes for the home cook like pozole, flan, and ceviche. Soon, she began to incorporate lessons about nutrition, and a call-in number flashed on the screen for viewers. They began to ask her advice on everything, from how to get a picky child to eat to cooking-related marital problems.

"Your husband suffers from an illness, which unfortunately many Mexican men suffer from," she counseled one woman. "It's called confusion. He doesn't know what a wife is, what a marriage is. What he wants is just to eat well. Help him: tell him to hire a very good cook so that he's treated as he deserves, to pay her very well so she'll stick around for a long time. Do it now, because confusion is contagious. You're already unsure if you got married to be a wife or to be an unpaid servant."

When Peralta cooked, it was clear she was having fun. She danced, chatted to the audience knowledgeably about prenatal health and child nutrition, and slowly removed her apron to the stylings of a saxophone—a light-hearted striptease. She passed away in 2021, at the age of 90.

Yuri de Gortari Krauss, who led a movement of appreciation for his country's culinary heritage, was equally quotable. "You know who is truly creative in the kitchen? The housewife," he declared, "because she cooks, a lot of the time, following suggestions from the fridge! She invents because she has to give good, nutritious, and attractive food to her kids. The rest of those chefs are just trying to catch a glimpse of their own reflection."

De Gortari, tall and skinny with a thick mustache and a penchant for bolo ties, opened La Bombilla with his husband, Edmundo Escamilla, in 1990. The couple was revolutionary in many ways, working and living as openly gay, and pioneering a scholarly homage to centuries-old Mexican cuisine. De Gortari was perhaps the most visible modern scholar of the country's gastronomic history, and eventually used that knowledge base when he opened Mexico's only cooking school dedicated entirely to the country's proprietary techniques, La Escuela de Gastronomía Mexicana. "People still don't consider the food we eat every day to be important enough for special events," he said. "It's shameful that we're here in Mexico, with the incredible diversity of food that we have, the culture of food that we have, and yet there's only one school specializing in Mexican cookery. It's regrettable. Through that example, you can see the ethnic shame we have in Mexico. Go to any cooking school here and you'll see that they instruct students in how to make a béchamel before they teach a *salsa de jitomate*."

The pre-Hispanic techniques taught at his school include the use of the *metate* and the molcajete, the comal and the clay oven, and how to use cornhusks to wrap tamales. Even techniques that appear to be hyper-modern can be traced to pre-Hispanic cooking: when de Gortari visited modern restaurants enamored of flavored foams, he looked to Zapotec chef Abigail Mendoza Ruiz, who makes chocolate atole by rapidly rolling the stick of a *molinillo*—a ridged wooden utensil with detached rings—between her palms to whisk air into the liquid until it transforms into a bounty of drinkable foam.

De Gortari shared many of his lessons in popular YouTube videos, before his death in 2020 of pancreatic cancer.

————

Lalo came back to Mexico largely unaware of the influences that preceded him. As his profile began to rise, he wasn't sure where his story fit into the larger narrative the media was building about Mexican fine dining, and he didn't know which details to amplify.

As Máximo approached its one-year anniversary, Alonso Ruvalcaba wrote a review in *Letras Libres,* a monthly literary magazine. He challenged the terms that dominated critical discussion of the restaurant's food, which, due to its emphasis on local and seasonal products, was often characterized as "simple" and "unpretentious." Ruvalcaba wanted the public to take a deeper look. Seasonal and local ingredients are to be expected in fine dining today, he wrote, and no, those ingredients don't determine the quality of the food— that's up to the chef who chooses how to prepare them. And while the food at Máximo may have given the impression of simplicity, when one plate is compared to another an artist of great range is revealed. Take, he suggested, the riotously colorful lobster aguachile, and place it alongside the restrained autumnal palate of roasted chicken and chanterelles. "It's luxurious," wrote Ruvalcaba. "And not just the ingredients that are chosen, but in how they are prepared. Fat, unctuousness, a sensation of fullness on the palate, *that's* luxury. (It's not luxury because they flew over the tuna from Tokyo, or because the utensils are made of gold, but really, does anyone still think that that's luxury?) In Mexico City today, there are few dishes as luxurious as the fried egg with sweetbreads at Máximo. It almost makes you feel guilty to eat something like that during these difficult times."

Those early reviews focused on seasonality and simplicity

because that was the primary story Lalo told—and he told it with conviction. To him, the ethic of farm-to-table food was rooted in a lifetime of experiences. It was in Mexico that he first tasted a criollo apple (what in the U.S. would be referred to as heirloom)—"the little ugly ones," apples that had defied generations of industrialization intent on mass-producing pretty, hearty varieties capable of traveling long distances unblemished so that they could be displayed in the aisles of a faraway supermarket.

During their years in the fields, Lalo and his family had been handed some of the produce they picked to take home at the end of each day. For the Garcías, that could add up to eight pints of berries, four kilos of apples, a flat of cucumbers. Even as a child, Lalo picked up on the differences in quality. Some of the cucumbers were plenty big, but they tasted like water. Others were small, their flesh snappy and sweet. The back of their Ford F-150 "was always full of buckets of apples, buckets of whatever we would pick." Sometimes, they'd meet up with other families and trade—cucumbers for tomatoes, raspberries for blackberries.

When Lalo began working at Pujol, he paid close attention to where they sourced their ingredients. This was the best restaurant in Mexico, so where did they get the best chocolate, corn, beans, oysters, pork? The answers weren't self-evident, even at Pujol. A salesman claimed to bring organic, traditionally grown products to the restaurant from the *chinampas* of Xochimilco, ancient man-made islands within the city limits, built from layers of mud and compost crisscrossed by canals. In the pre-Hispanic era, Xochimilco was known for having the cleanest, most plentiful water close to the Aztec capital of Tenochtitlan, and the area was an agricultural center where crops thrived in the dark, nutrient-rich soil. Lucio Usobiaga was a college student when he began working with the salesman,

excited to be part of a business connecting the chinampas with restaurants. But Usobiaga quickly realized that the salesman was lying
about his source. In fact, he was buying almost everything from the
Central de Abasto, and it was easy enough to detect the fraud: pine-
apples, for example, didn't grow in the chinampas. The chefs of the
day weren't deeply involved in the way their ingredients were grown,
so they believed him.

Usobiaga saw an opportunity to get involved. The future of the
chinampas was uncertain: housing developments threatened to
overtake the land, and once that occurred it was unlikely they'd ever
return to their traditional use. Here was an ecological paradise, full
of wildlife, and a place to grow local food that had somehow survived
urban sprawl in the continent's most populated city. He knew from
the beginning he was doing something transcendent, even though
the farming life was still new to him as the son of an industrial
engineer and an English teacher in Mexico City. Not many of the
chinamperos wanted to plant organic—if the new technique didn't
work, they'd be left with no crop to sell—and he struggled to convince them otherwise. "Why would they listen to a *guerito* from the
city telling them what to plant?"

The farmers knew that there were high-end restaurants in the
city and chefs who wanted to find a reliable source of organic, specialized produce, but they needed more than a networking opportunity. The pace of their work didn't afford them the time to solicit
meetings, much less retool their operations to pursue the more ambitious strategy of planting to accommodate a given chef's anticipated
menu, two or three months in the future. They needed a salesper-
son to do the time-consuming work of convincing restaurateurs and
later, subscribers to a weekly produce box, to value their products
and pay more for them. Usobiaga filled that role.

When Máximo opened, Lalo became one of Usobiaga's best clients, and he began to visit the chinampas on a regular basis. He'd board a *trajinera*, a flat-bottomed wooden boat, at 6 a.m., just as the sun began its ascent, the division between water and sky a blur of orange-tinted fog. He personally harvested what he wanted to take back to the restaurant and took stock of what would be available a week or a month down the road, and how he might use it on his menu.

For Mexican chefs, including products from the chinampas is about more than the philosophy of eating local and organic. It's a way to tell the story of Mexico, to hint, via an ingredient, a geographic term, an ancient farming method, at the extent of the history that's embedded in that delicious bite. Máximo Bistrot was one of a small cluster of critically acclaimed restaurants to open around the same time, all dedicated to these principles, with Pujol as the vanguard and later Rosetta (circa 2010) and Quintonil (circa 2012). Quintonil, headed by chef Jorge Vallejo, frequently features native produce like the restaurant's namesake wild greens, which waiters take time to explain tableside. At Rosetta, chef Elena Reygadas is adept at bringing forward some of the country's less obviously luxurious ingredients and includes them in elegant tableaus. Take the composed dessert of *nanches** in syrup, pickled yucca flowers, lemon ice cream, and nanche sorbet, with a sour cream and lemon panna cotta, elements which are layered together on the plate in shades of yellow, peach, and white. In her cookbook she explains that "the most demanding and least complacent ingredients are the ones I find most satisfying when we manage to make them shine," a challenge that

---

* The *nanche* is a small, pungent yellow fruit with a sweet-sour flavor that's sometimes described as cheese-like. Nanches grow on a large shrub and have many names, including craboo, yaca, *nance*, golden spoon, hogberry, *chaparro de sabana*, *maricao cimaroon*, *paralejo blanco*, *changugu*, and *doncela*.

pays off in recognition of a neglected product and the discovery of a new use for it. Here, the fattiness of the cream and the aroma of the lemon "act as bridges between the sweetness of the nanche in syrup and the acidity of the yucca flowers."

For Olvera, there's another, more basic reason to use local products: they taste better. In France, you might seek out the best-quality escargots and tarragon; in Mexico, the *escamoles*, or ant eggs, are top of the line. Olvera never set out to extol *pápalo*, a variety of peppery, herbaceous wild greens. Rather, he was drawn to them as a young cook searching through local markets for the best raw materials. Usobiaga inaugurated an annual fundraiser—la Cena por las Chinampas—in 2017. Olvera, Vallejo, Reygadas, and Lalo, along with Gabriela Cámara of Contramar, teamed up to cook in an ex-convent in downtown Mexico City, and each year the proceeds benefit the effort to restore traditional farming methods.

While this burgeoning movement has been successful in creating a renewed appreciation for tortillas made with landrace corn, the possibilities of the tamal (of which there are thousands of varieties) and the delicacy of certain insects, it also came about at a moment when the nation's farmers had been driven away from nurturing those crops, leading to a loss of biodiversity and traditional foodways. In her book *Eating NAFTA: Trade, Food Policies, and the Destruction of Mexico*, anthropologist Alyshia Gálvez details the ways in which economic policy, along with land privatization and industrialization, have rapidly conspired to make ancestral diets challenging to maintain. For someone living in rural Puebla, it can be difficult to find fresh produce for sale, but a Coke and a bag of chips, with their long shelf life and aggressive corporate push into Mexican communities, are ubiquitous. Paradoxically, Gálvez writes, this estrangement from native foodways in rural Mexico is what enables high-end chefs in elite environments to "elevate" endangered foods. As heirloom beans or chicatana ants become scarcer, it's easier to convince a comparatively wealthy audience to pay top dollar, further warping the price of these foods for local communities. It's not that the chefs are ill-intentioned; on the contrary, Reygadas and Vallejo, Lalo and Olvera support small farmers vocally and actively. They've pushed awareness of traditional methods and the quality of the products into public discourse, and source their ingredients from local purveyors, embracing "ugly" produce and cooking for free at fundraising events.

Still, it can feel as though subterranean magnets are pulling these gains in the opposite direction: the environment is further polluted when eco-resorts move into once pristine areas, flooding the cenotes of the Yucatán with tourists and the sewage their presence generates. A reforestation program, Sowing Life, created by the government of President Andrés Manuel López Obrador, perversely prompted the deforestation of an area the size of New York City by giving campesinos money to grow certain types of trees; the program created a financial incentive to cut down other varieties of old-growth trees and plant saplings of the approved species.

Biodiverse corn, the critical ingredient in Mexican cuisine, has been one of the most consequential losses as a result of NAFTA. According to the logic that guided the accord, crops should be grown where they are most productive by conventional measures. The U.S., where farmers were protected by corn subsidies, quadrupled its exports of corn to Mexico after the agreement's ratification. In Mexico, where landrace corn adapted over thousands of years to specific microclimates, yielding varieties in a rainbow of colors and flavors, farmers were incentivized to switch to other crops, or abandon the milpa system altogether. Millions of rural Mexicans moved to border cities like Reynosa, Matamoros, and Tijuana to work in assembly plants, or migrated to the United States to work on industrialized farms and in slaughterhouses, or to the Estado de México in search of work in construction, manufacturing, and restaurants. By the time ethanol came to be a major market force, global corn prices rose, spurring protests over the cost of tortillas in Mexico. Today, the corn flour market is dominated by Gruma, which owns Mission tortillas and Maseca flour. Simultaneously, processed food has become a cheap, compulsively available part of the Mexican diet. As nutritious drinks like atole have become less common, Mexico has come to claim the highest per capita soda consumption in the world.

This isn't the first time in Mexico's postcolonial history that the tortilla has come under threat. As early as the sixteenth century, when Spain imported its exploitative *encomienda* system (in which white settlers entrusted with vast swaths of land in New Spain could require tribute from indigenous peoples, often in the form of forced labor, which was, according to the system's logic, "exchanged" for protection and Catholic indoctrination), Europeans attempted to bring wheat to New Spain, viewing corn with suspicion. In 1899, author and politician Francisco Bulnes published a manifesto dividing mankind into three categories, according to the wheat, rice, or corn they primarily consumed. Corn was, according to Bulnes, nutritionally inferior. The categorization of people via grains was another manifestation of the broader eugenics discourse gaining momentum around the turn of the century. Scientists would ultimately conclude that the nutritional value of corn had been underestimated. The supposed nutritional deficiency of the tortilla was a distraction, as historian Jeffrey Pilcher explains, from the centuries of disenfranchisement suffered by the country's indigenous population, who were forcibly separated from their land. By 1910, the dawn of the Mexican Revolution, the vast majority of Mexico's rural land

was owned by a fraction of the population, and it had become difficult if not impossible for many people to grow and gather the necessary components for the healthy diet that had historically sustained
them. The ruling class understood that corn was "the root of a self-
supporting communal life," Pilcher writes; severing that root would
force campesinos to modernize.

At Pujol, Olvera has promoted landrace corn, demonstrating
to his customers (primarily foreign tourists and wealthy Mexicans), the difference it makes in the flavor and quality of a tortilla.
This approach has been adapted by his protégés. Today it would be
strange to encounter a tortilla made with mass-produced masa in any
high-end Mexico City restaurant. Put in the parlance of the elite, the
landrace, nixtamalized tortilla is now gourmet, heirloom, artisanal.

"Is gentrification of anything inherently bad?" Gálvez wondered
aloud. "I think there is a way that elevation produces value for things
that have otherwise been snubbed or devalued." Maybe this could
spur a beneficial chain reaction, "so that people with less access to
that elite stratosphere can grow corn and expect to sell it and have
chinampas and expect to have a market for it. There is a ripple effect
that produces something a thousand times better than the NAFTA
economy of processed foods going back and forth across the border."
Still, she said, such an impact would only have value if those institu-
tions honor the communities from which those products come, and
ensure that they are getting a cut.

In her desire to promote mezcal in the dining room of Naos,
chef Mónica Patiño inadvertently helped to kick off a process that
would drastically raise the price of maguey, from 30 centavos for a
kilo of espadín in 2005, to around 14 pesos a kilo as of this writing. That may have initially been a good thing for the farmers who
cultivate maguey, but production for export has already shifted to

a group of large companies—José Cuervo, Patrón, Bacardi—with profits siphoned thusly. Meanwhile, mezcal is rapidly becoming too costly for most Oaxacans to consume as they once did. "The Oaxacan people were the first to stop drinking mezcal," said one master distiller, preferring to keep her name out of print due to safety concerns; criticizing the region's cash-cow can be perilous. "Beyond the change in price, the quest for money and fame is tearing our communities apart," pitting family members against one another as conflicts over land use, sustainability, and foreign investment escalate. Mezcal fever also raises concerns about how sustainable it can possibly be to produce distillations from wild varieties of maguey that require decades to come to maturity, or to grow maguey in mass quantities in regions that are suffering from water shortages. Gálvez says she remembers a time when she visited Oaxaca and mezcaleros could barely give the beverage away—they were doing their best to convince tourists to at least try a sample during an open-air market.

"It's very particular people who can be those 'pioneers,'" Gálvez said—those who speak the language of the elite and also have a deep understanding of the value of the products themselves. Chefs are a natural fit: they move between the dining room, the kitchen, and the environs of purveyors. Increasingly, they are then asked to explain the connections between a country's food, people, history, and environment.

Olvera says he wants Mexico to properly value its assets, that there ought to be room for a range of experiences and price points— the taco you eat on the street and the one you eat in his dining room, with lobster of the same quality as what is served at Ripert's Le Bernardin. But when landrace corn is valued according to the terms of the free market, which is today a global market suddenly enamored of what was once a low-cost resource, there is an inherent risk that it will become more distant from its communities of origin, in the manner of the primary materials for making mezcal. The tortilla, as Gálvez writes, doesn't need to put on airs or be extolled abroad to have value. "It is and has been enough all by itself."

———————

In 2018, Luis Usobiaga started a series of dinners in which cooks visit the *chinampa del sol* in Xochimilco and prepare a multi-course feast using the ingredients found on site. They cook on a wood-powered stove, and there's plenty of Mexican wine, beer, and mezcal for celebrating. The real purpose of the meals is not celebration but publicity: he wants people to subscribe to the weekly produce box. The sales pitch draws its strength from the showcasing of the quality of the produce on offer and the simultaneous intelligence and precariousness of the chinampa methodology. Demand for boxes from his group, now called Arca Tierra, is growing, but relatively few of Xochimilco's chinampas are being used for farming, and there's potential to scale up. He's not the only child of the city trying to find a way to support local agriculture. Francisco Musi, the cofounder of Tamoa, works with small farmers across the country to bring their organically grown landrace corn, beans, and chiles to consumers at four or five times what they'd fetch in the open market. Musi jokes that if you told someone with an MBA that you planned to source micro-quantities from hundreds of family farms across eight states, they'd think you were crazy, but that's precisely what Tamoa does. Biodiversity is idiosyncratic, and therefore so is the business model.

Lalo's passion for seeking out these products made Máximo stand out from day one. It took time, but he found the country's best supplier of organic, free-range chicken, and a diver who drives in his shellfish, tuna and sardines from the Oaxacan coast. He found sources of sustainable cheese, eggs, wine, potatoes, and cacao, hailing from the arid Baja peninsula to the jungles of Chiapas. Some purveyors met Lalo after waiting for hours on the sidewalk until service ended, using a cooler full of spiny lobsters as a bench. Others contacted him on Instagram. Whenever possible, he personally visited the farm or the vineyard or the mountainside where they grew their coffee beans, dug their potatoes, harvested their grapes. Lalo came to see this as the main distinction between Máximo and other restaurants: the integrity of the ingredients, each one verified by the person in charge of the kitchen, a person with intimate knowledge of not only how to prepare food, but how it is grown. For years, Michele Sedgwick had shared her passion for quality ingredients, and, along with it, her concerns about the dangers of pesticides, GMOs, and homogenous agriculture. A pushback against the mainstream food system was growing, from Alice Waters's Chez Panisse to Italy's Slow Food movement. After spending his childhood in his grandparents' milpa and the industrialized fields of the U.S., Lalo understood these principles at his core. He became more selective about what he put in his body and, in his role of selecting food for his customers, was committed to serving only what he himself would eat.

In the chinampas, Lalo found a homecoming to a place he'd never known as a child. Sailing slowly through the canals on a wooden trajinera cleared his mind and prepared him for the day ahead. It was the closest he could come to explaining his creative process, a reconnection with the earth and the milpa that rekindled his imagination and gave him reserves of energy. When he was feeling depressed, angry, exhausted, he looked to the chinampas for renewal the way someone else might recommit themselves to attending church or following a low-carb diet. "I should start going every morning," he'd say to Gaby. In reality, one or two trips a month were all he could manage. Going to Arca Tierra's chinampas required an hour's commute each way by car and boat. Only then could he spend a precious hour harvesting kale, fennel, and lettuce, as sunshine touched the golden tassel on a young corn stalk, crept across the black earth, and electrified the mist.

"People who don't have that relationship to the countryside, they say, 'how pretty,'" Usobiaga said. "For Lalo, visiting the chinampas awakens memories, it awakens dreams."

The delicacy and importance of local food was the guiding story at Máximo Bistrot for good reason. And it might have stayed that way forever if someone else hadn't shown up at the door and hijacked the narrative. They called her Lady Profeco.

CHAPTER EIGHT

LADY PROFECO

IT HAD BEEN a year and a half since Máximo opened, and business was booming, when Andrea Benítez González, a young socialite, walked through the door and asked to be seated. All the tables were reserved, Gaby explained, but added her name to the wait list. As of yet, there was no lounge area, and Benítez loitered on the sidewalk with a friend, though they had no drinks or appetizers to help pass the time. As Gaby would recall years later, Benítez began to question each of Gaby's decisions from her post on the concrete. Why was there a woman sitting alone surrounded by five empty chairs? Why couldn't she have that table? "I'm sorry," Gaby told her, "that woman is a very good customer and she has a reservation. There's nothing I can do."

More than an hour had passed when Benítez spotted waiters clearing a two-top outside. Her name was next on the wait list and she asked Gaby if she could head to the table. "No, I'm sorry," said Gaby, though her tone had grown curt. Gaby needed to accommodate a loyal customer who had asked to switch to an outdoor table so he could smoke. Benítez would be seated indoors. Benítez protested, insisting the table should be hers.

After a decade of working for other people, Gaby managed her restaurant with pride. In the short term, it seemed that she could afford to stand up to pushy customers: the reservation book was full, and people lined up on the sidewalk in hopes someone wouldn't show. When Benítez began to chime in as a one-woman peanut gallery, Gaby grew impatient.

"I almost said, 'When you have *your* restaurant you can do whatever you want.' Because there are a lot of guests who say, 'Why don't you put this here, and you could put these two tables here.' I'm like, this is *my* restaurant, I can do whatever I want!"

As Gaby showed her to the indoor table, she heard Benítez talking into her cell phone about her poor treatment and demanding that inspectors be sent to the restaurant.

Gaby knew that the "inspectors" would be from the country's consumer protection agency, Profeco. Máximo was still in a drawn-out process of getting its paperwork in order, and Gaby went to the kitchen in a panic. "There's a woman being super rude," she told Lalo. "She's saying she's going to get us inspected!" Lalo called over Oscar, the manager, to deliver a message:

"Oscar, please tell this lady that we will not serve her today. We heard that she wants to send us an inspection and I'm all about feelings and emotions, and I don't feel like cooking for her anymore."

Oscar walked a few yards to Benítez, who was finally settled at her long-awaited table. He delivered a version of Lalo's message. The match had been struck.

Benitez left in a huff. Her father, Humberto Benítez Treviño, was the director of Profeco, and she promised they'd be hearing from him.

Then, Benítez fired off a tweet:

"*Pésimo servicio, no tienen educación . . . No volvería nunca.*" Dreadful service, they have no manners. I'd never go back there. Shortly after, she posted her location on FourSquare: the Profeco agency.

Gaby felt like she'd made a hubristic mistake.

Benítez was hardly the first angry customer in that inaugural year. As word spread about the in-demand tables at Máximo, the city's wealthiest residents from neighborhoods like Polanco, Santa Fe, and Lomas came to a corner of the Roma their families hadn't visited since the 1985 earthquake laid ruin to its fine homes and businesses. On their side of the city, they were accustomed to treating waiters like a temporary staff of personal servants. At Máximo, Gaby overheard their insults before she had even shown them to their seats: "What is this *pinche* fonda?" they'd remark as they peeked in the door. "They don't even have tablecloths, what are we doing here?"

Gaby's family had scrimped and saved to send her to a private school with privileged girls like Benítez. Back then, she was desperate to create the impression that she had more money than she really did. She invented a chauffeur and a country house. Later, she was embarrassed by these fibs. Surely her classmates didn't believe them, anyway: the chauffeur never materialized when she needed a ride. Mostly, Gaby was ashamed. She'd been so focused on fitting in, she'd neglected to show gratitude for the blessings her sacrificing parents had laboriously bestowed.

As an adult, Gaby found herself caught between the twin forces of a career in hospitality: the desire to create an experience that is genuinely beautiful and pleasing for strangers, and the money that ultimately undergirds the entire system. In her travels, Gaby had come to appreciate the concept of a European-style bistro: it was not just the small menus and intimate layout that she wanted to replicate, but what she saw as its heart: the relationship between proprietor and client, as embodied by the owner who stands at the door to warmly welcome the customer, especially the regular customer, into this second home. The owner who ensures that all the details— from the temperature of the wine to the volume of the music—meet her standards. To Gaby, the restaurant was an extension of her and Lalo's home. She expected some basic etiquette from their guests. When entitled customers met her at that door with insults, she took them personally.

"And we're like, 'If you don't want to stay, you don't need to stay!'" This wasn't a silent thought that ran through Gaby's mind; it was literally what she told them. Eventually, some diners stopped coming. They were replaced by tourists, along with regulars who mainly hailed from the adjacent neighborhoods. The floor managers remained eager to eject rude customers. Gaby told them that the customers had changed, and they had to as well. We're not doing them a favor, she said. They're doing us a favor by coming.

So, on that fateful afternoon, Benítez was the latest in a long line of attackers; she met Gaby at the end of a frayed rope. The exchange unfolded breathlessly, without a moment of strategic talk between Gaby and Lalo. Later, Gaby would look at every prickly customer with this hard-won hindsight: kill them with kindness. Maybe if she'd been more apologetic, less arrogant, the whole incident could have been avoided. "I should have said, 'I'm so sorry madame, I really apologize, we will make it up to you. We will do our best, please let me offer you a cocktail.'"

Sure enough, the Profeco inspectors came by with their massive red and white stickers in search of an offense. They looked through the kitchen, pored over the menus. Profeco cited irregularities in the restaurant's reservation system and the unauthorized sale of certain types of mezcal—a carefully controlled beverage in Mexico requiring an official seal to qualify for the title of "mezcal." One of the diners observing the spectacle was a lawyer, who asked Gaby if she needed help. Soon, his team descended on the restaurant and went head to head with the inspectors.

Customers took videos. Benítez had unwittingly substantiated the forthcoming claim of corruption with her tweets. #LadyProfeco started trending, holding up Benítez as the incarnation of corrupt elites who use their status to cut the lines that other Mexicans must abide. As the confrontation reached a fever pitch, neighbors came out into the street. Then, when the dinner service began, a new crop of diners began to ask Gaby what all the fuss was about. One offered to call the newspapers. In the heat of the moment, she agreed, and was soon giving an interview to *Reforma*. By Sunday, the saga was splashed across the front pages of Mexico's national newspapers. It would be covered by *El País* and the BBC.

"To many of its fans, the restaurant is the Chez Panisse of Mexico City, a gastro-paradise of fresh ingredients delivered with innovation for (relatively) affordable prices, in a simple dining room often populated by stars, from Mexican actors to visiting luminaries like Patti Smith," Damien Cave wrote in the *New York Times*. Max St. Romain, a filmmaker, told Cave the incident connected to "the corruption that ruled Mexico for decades—the fact that a child of someone in power can use it just on a whim, on a tantrum."

But as they took the spotlight, Gaby and Lalo regretted everything. Gaby told her lawyers to make it all go away, even as the phone exploded with interview requests. The next day, business went on as usual, but as press coverage continued to build, they decided to close temporarily in a desperate attempt to calm things down. When Máximo reopened its doors, TV news reporters did stand-ups on the corner of Zacatecas and Tonalá, informing the public about the coveted

reservation list and the charming young couple's fight against institutional corruption. Overnight, as #LadyProfeco became a meme and
cast Benítez as a spoiled villain of the upper class, Lalo and Gaby
became unwitting martyrs—the small business owners struggling
to do right in a rigged system.

The incident pushed on a pressure point, revealing national angst
about entitlement and social class. Lalo and Gaby weren't eager to
take up the role of activists; in Mexico, having a spotlight shined on
your success or speaking out against the government might win you
points, but it could also come back to bite you. Yes, they tried to pay
their workers well, source locally, give their time to good causes. But
ultimately they wanted to have a profitable, successful business and
that success depended on the upper class, the people with the money
to pay for caviar and truffles and bottles of expensive wine.

The federal government launched an investigation. #LadyProfe-
co's father lost his job, along with four other officials in the consumer
protection agency. Gaby and Lalo thought the incident was behind
them, and that they had somehow escaped the promised wrath of
Profeco. But over the coming months and years, they would get more
than the usual dose of attention from the agency, which smacked,
again and again, their embarrassing stickers on the restaurant's windows and walls for offenses like offering a customer a cup of soup
when only a bowl was priced on the written menu.

The next year, Anthony Bourdain visited Máximo Bistrot for
his CNN show *Parts Unknown*, in a segment framed around young
restaurateurs in Mexico who were fighting corruption. While Lalo
and Gaby might have been privately uncomfortable with the activist
image that was forced on them, publicly they embraced it.

"Eduardo García has hacked his way up the ladder to become
chef-owner of the city's hottest restaurant," says Bourdain, wear-

ing a beige linen blazer and standing at the marble counter, where Lalo serves him a taco of suckling pig confit with salsa tatemada—basically, Lalo's take on carnitas. Bourdain holds a knife and fork over the plate; he hesitates. Have at it, Lalo tells him. Bourdain collects the taco in his right hand, assesses the drip factor with an up-and-down jiggle, leans over, and takes a bite.

"Wow," Bourdain says. "Pretty hard to imagine anything better than that. You're stuck with this dish forever, man. It's going to be like Mick Jagger fifty years from now, singing 'Satisfaction.' There's no getting away from it man, this is so good! This is a classic." For Lalo, who worshipped Bourdain, it was the greatest compliment of his life.

Lalo tells Bourdain about the corruption that rules Mexico. "You have to stand up for what you believe—if you don't, people will run you over. You won't last a minute. I don't let people bully me around." The threats, the class condescension, were a daily fact of life, but he wouldn't let someone like Lady Profeco determine his fate. "I'd rather close my restaurant than live like that." Maybe he'd be forced to move across the street, or maybe he'd be pushed into another country. He wouldn't give in.

Lady Profeco confirmed for Lalo the dark side of the country his parents had left behind. When he was forced to make a new beginning, he'd had a streak of good luck: a great job, love, a year at the beach and then a new restaurant all his own that was a raving success within months of its opening day. But here was the rigged system in action, embodied by the wealth, privilege, and outright corruption of Lady Profeco, requiring masses of low-paid, exploited workers to make it all possible.

Lalo paid close attention to the news. With his roster of connected customers, he was often the first to get a message when a plane had crashed or a politician made a gaffe. He was watching as deportations of Mexicans from the U.S. began to accelerate during the Obama administration, and the coverage of parents and children afraid to return to a country that was now unfamiliar. Then, a man who had spent a lifetime building a façade of success by gambling with his father's money launched his presidential bid with a speech about a wall that would extend across the southern border to protect the U.S. from bogeymen.

"When Mexico sends its people," Donald Trump infamously told a crowd as he announced his presidential candidacy, "they're not sending their best. They're not sending you. They're not sending you. They're sending people that have lots of problems, and they're bringing those problems with us. They're bringing drugs. They're bringing crime. They're rapists. And some, I assume, are good people."

A few days after Trump won, Lalo was standing in the kitchen of Máximo watching a video on Instagram of *"el nuevo deporte Meji-cano"*: four athletes sprint along a track toward a wall with a ladder in their hands; they throw it up against the wall and climb three stories to the top. The winner scales the wall in just over twelve seconds. Lalo laughed and shook his head. After all, didn't he perfectly fit Trump's definition of the "bad hombre": a convicted felon who had been living in the country without permission, and had made multiple illegal entries without much fuss? Lalo was just the sort of person that the extended border wall was intended to keep out. Among Máximo's staff, everyone knew his story. In a Mexican restaurant kitchen, it wasn't terribly unique. He shared his memories and then listened as his employees recounted their own border crossings, their time working alongside famed chefs in kitchens across the U.S., their homecomings to Mexico.

In those early post-election days, Lalo dismissed Trump as just another con, not altogether different from Mexico's then president,

Enrique Peña Nieto. By the time Trump was elected, Peña Nieto had an approval rating of 17 percent. Lalo often dreamed about becoming Mexico's president. But his methods, he said, would be extreme. To fight corruption, he'd have to root out the ten or fifteen families that rule Mexico, and to do that you'd need the support of a highly advanced army. He'd build prisons instead of roads, "prisons where you forget about people."

Sometimes politicians and their children would come to dine at Máximo. Sometimes members of the ten or fifteen families came in. Gaby and Lalo regarded them more or less equally: people who might become loyal customers. But they were also people who could turn on them and use their clout to harm, as they had learned all too well; therefore, they must be kept at a careful distance.

In January of 2017, a British couple came into the restaurant and complained to their waiter that there were no budget options on the wine list. As they were leaving, Gaby stopped to ask the woman about her meal. The portions were too small, she complained, and the wine wasn't good. At first Gaby apologized: you should have told us how you felt! We would have served you more food or changed the wine. But the woman was already upset. "She said, 'I think we're going to do what Donald Trump says, and we're going to shut the doors to Mexico and we're not coming back.' And I'm like, how can you say that? And I said, 'I think a person who thinks like you shouldn't come to Mexico, so I'm glad you're not coming back.'"

The episode shook Gaby. More than the anger and embarrassment she had felt with Lady Profeco, she felt grief. Gaby had grown up with elite Mexicans and she knew they could be snobs. But this was a new variation on a well-established trend—the phenomenon of foreigners who come to Mexico expecting everything to be cheap, who were newly emboldened by populist racism, emboldened by a president who earned political points every time he degraded Mexico.

Lalo fell into grief when a man around his age, Guadalupe Olivas Valencia, committed suicide by jumping from an international bridge linking San Diego with Tijuana, less than an hour after being denied entry to the United States. He had worked as a gardener there for years. A few days later, an interview with Lalo ran in the *New York Times*, mostly composed of direct quotes: a "bad hombre" tale, as the reporter wrote, of a famed chef who could no longer come to the United States. Lalo told the newspaper that he wanted "to encourage Mexicans who are in the same situation to know they'll be welcome to come back and be in their own country."

Lalo didn't know much about Valencia, but what he knew nagged at him: he was a working-class person, like himself, who had decided to end his life rather than return to Mexico. It was suddenly clear to him that this story—his story—might be able to make some other deportee feel less alone. He wondered if sharing his story could save someone, too.

CHAPTER NINE

EL JEFE

THROUGHOUT THE MORNING prep, people tapped on the door and asked for Lalo: an Insta-famous foodie from Japan, a purveyor of chocolate hoping for a new customer, a Scottish cook asking if he could stage in the kitchen for a few months. Lalo cut away the moldy exterior from an aged ribeye, then pivoted to a gripe session with the wait staff about politics. He'd sing snatches of songs by Paul Simon and Consuelo Velázquez and dance in his cramped two square feet of the galley kitchen.

During service, he was forever at the pass, the bridge between the more monotonous tasks of the kitchen and the hedonism of the dining room. He plated every entrée himself. Lalo had a natural talent for turning a collection of ingredients into a cohesive, beautiful composition. Sauces in shades of light brown, forgettable smudges of mud when spooned on the plate by a different hand, were recast as earth tones that heightened the intense orange of a roasted carrot, the blush in the crisp skin of red snapper. On black pottery, tentacles of seared octopus glowed next to pools of beans and *mole negro*. He'd

finish a dish with a sprinkle of the flowering tips of cilantro, like a
Renaissance-era rendition of lace.

The morning would begin with the quiet hum of just a few cooks
embarking on the first steps of the day's most intensive preparations.
By midday, the space was full. Each cook, stationed in front of the
range or the stainless steel counters, had just enough room to pivot
in three directions. The fires lit up, the temperature climbed. The
cooks were alert as they listened to Lalo's instructions and as he cor-
rected their technique. As they worked, the threat of his change-
able temperament loomed. When mistakes and then more mistakes
were made, their eyes would focus on their respective tasks, their
spines tipped low like spindly pine trees away from the approaching
thunderclouds.

From outside the fray, the whirl of simultaneous activity was
dazzling to watch. Lalo, though broad, usually managed to move
through the scrum without so much as losing a drop of hollandaise
to the floor. He plunged spoons in and out of plastic containers as he
assembled the plates, using a microplane to shave macadamia nuts
over a risotto, assertively grinding pepper onto a towering salad, putting a few large grains of salt just-so on the thick slices of a ribeye.
Lalo loved to send out free plates of food—ceviche and tostadas to
start, a slice of French toast with blueberry compote and vanilla ice
cream to finish. He didn't discriminate. Regular customers, first-time
tourists, a table of cooking students from the sticks who'd scrimped
and saved for their celebratory graduation meal, all were caught off
guard by the approach of a waiter with an unanticipated dish. Before
they left, they'd come by to pay their respects to the chef, and were
met with an elbow bump and a half-smile. Lalo barely acknowledged
these gifts. Anyway, he was too immersed in cooking to entertain
conversation. Unless it was a child curious to hear about an ingredi-

ent. Or a fruit vendor passing by on a hot day. "Tell him we'll buy
the whole cart," he'd instruct a waiter. "We'll make *agua de mango*."
Then, he'd offer the salesman a cold drink and a *pan dulce*.

Employees were happy to share their stories about Lalo. How, on
slow days, he'd take them to eat at a friend's new restaurant. How he
and Gaby would send clothes and toys home with an employee who
was welcoming a new baby. How they paid for funerals when a staff
member needed help burying a loved one with dignity.

There was the staff field trip they organized to the village of
Acatepec, where many of the waiters were from, renting a bus and
driving ten hours round-trip. There, the group toured an ancient salt
mine and a cactus garden, and ended the day with a sunset pig roast
at the ranch that one of their first hires, Oscar, had built up over the
years. When extreme rains destroyed the boats that bartender Federico Ríos's family depended on for their livelihood, they matched
donations to buy new ones. There were fundraisers for people they
didn't even know: the artisans in Chiapas, the low-income students
at Gastromotiva who were earning cooking certificates. For the vic-
tims of an earthquake in Morelos, Lalo couldn't just write a check;
he and his staff prepared a truckload of food and sent the company
van off to pass out meals in rural parks and churches to people who
had lost their homes.

Each year, Lalo and Gaby held a Christmas party. There was food
and cake and plenty of booze, and each member of the staff got a
raffled-off gift with a bottle of something to take home to continue
the celebration with their family. Gaby stood up in front of the group
and gave a speech. "For us, to have a team like you and be able to provide work for so many people, is the greatest thing. I love to be able
to do this for you, I hope you enjoy it as much as I do. I do it because I
love you all very much. That's all. Merry Christmas, I hope you have

wonderful celebrations, and how incredible to be able to share them with our families. I hope that next year is even better for everyone." When they got to the final prizes in the raffle—a flat-screen TV and an iPad—there were alcohol-fueled games of musical chairs on Calle Zacatecas to determine the winner. The street echoed with laughter and hooting. Gaby danced in the middle of the celebration, giggling with wet eyes and red cheeks. Some workers headed to the sous-chef's apartment to continue the party. Lalo returned to the kitchen of Máximo to finish his work for the night.

———

While some members of the staff had stayed on for years, Lalo worried constantly about divisions within his ranks, and searched for signs of weakness or mutiny. This suspicion was directed at nearly everyone: the other restaurateurs he counted as peers or dismissed as posers, the people working for him in the kitchen and on the floor, the reporter who came by for an interview, even some of the customers. Most often, eating out with him was no fun: apart from a handful of chefs and protégés he admired, the only cooks who received his praise were the home cooks in his life—Gaby and, when she visited, Natalia, along with his favorite purveyor of quesadillas. Since opening Máximo, Lalo and Gaby had launched two more restaurants: Havre 77, with classical French cuisine and a raw bar, and Lalo!, a popular brunch spot, whose menu would have been equally at home in Brooklyn or San Francisco: avocado toast, green juice, an açai bowl with seasonal fruit, pizza and pasta specials. Together, the three establishments were led by a handful of longtime employees.

Juan Escalona Meléndez, a young scientist from the Estado de Mexico, had been drawn away from his studies in chemistry at the University of Leeds to cook. He worked at Máximo for six months.

Escalona had worked for chefs obsessed either with growth and profit, or with their restaurant's concept and its role in an ever-changing cultural landscape. But Lalo seemed to care only about the act of preparing food well. He was always there. "He only left maybe when he was completely worn out, incredibly tired or angry—then he'd leave." As soon as Lalo arrived he'd perceive everything—the work that was going apace and the tiniest mistakes. At first, Escalona tried to hide his small errors in the interest of getting the rest of his work done on time, but he soon learned this wasn't possible. "Once, I was in the pass with him and I went to put parmesan on three or four risottos. So there was a moment when I turned quickly and grated a little of the rind onto the plate and then I covered it with more cheese. He saw me and said, 'You don't know what you're doing with that parmesan.' And he told me, 'Sometimes I think you can be so smart, or such an idiot.'"

Some people heard these comments and internally rolled their eyes. Others wanted to prove Lalo wrong. For Escalona? They made him want to leave. Escalona's interest in food was deep and far-ranging. He happily performed months-long experiments fermenting carrots and corn and studied the philosophy of aesthetics as it pertains to food, admiring Jean Anthelme Brillat-Savarin's *The Physiology of Taste* ("tell me what you eat and I shall tell you what you are"). Escalona wanted to examine food with the rigor applied to the art forms of painting and music, with careful attention to its historical, philosophical, and scientific applications. His small apartment was a laboratory of sorts, sparsely appointed apart from his culinary tools, including a temperature- and humidity-controlled ex-refrigerator where he cultivated koji—a type of mold used in fermentation—and a derelict Mexicana airline cart stuffed with spices (his father once worked for the airline). Escalona had spent a year cooking under

René Redzepi at Noma in Copenhagen, considered by many to be the best restaurant on Earth, known for its relentless experimentation and Redzepi's commitment to foraging for underutilized foods, like sea aster and black currant leaves. Staff at Noma, who journeyed to Denmark from across the globe, were also asked to share their own creativity during the weekly ritual of Saturday Night Projects. Even though he ranked at the lowest level of seniority at Noma, Escalona felt that his perspective was valued. Likewise, as a graduate student in Leeds, he had cold-called Nobel Prize winners and found them happy to entertain his questions. It didn't take long for him to realize that Lalo's stamp of approval was more elusive.

Escalona devoted the same geeky obsession to Máximo as he had to learning genomic biology. He watched Lalo's technique with profound admiration and came to work ready to learn. The repertoire at Máximo had evolved over the years, but that wasn't obvious to the untrained eye. It took a fanatic like Escalona to appreciate the subtle changes taking place within Lalo's tight, well-honed oeuvre, built on a foundation of umami and butter. In Escalona's mind, Máximo's menu was made up of a mathematically discrete set of elements: a protein cooked to perfection, purees, vegetables that complement and complicate. Technique was where the evolution occurred. Lalo constantly sought out better products and methods and adapted accordingly.

When Escalona arrived at Máximo, his mild-mannered disposition masked an ambitious set of hopes. He was desperate for Lalo to see him as a worthy mentee and an asset, who could work as a partner to expand the restaurant's canon. At his job interview, Escalona expressed interest in fermentation and composting, and Lalo was encouraging: they'd embark on a new project with Escalona at the helm. But for whichever among half a dozen reasons—not enough time, not enough interest, not enough space—that never came to pass.

Escalona started his own project, El Sexto Colectivo, in 2018, a multidisciplinary group interested in exploring food from every angle. One member was a budding restaurateur, another worked in marketing, another was a pharmaceutical researcher. They met periodically to research concepts both concrete and abstract: fermentation, fish, form. Then, they put on pop-up meals that embodied what they'd learned together. He'd never been so happy: he had found a group of friends who were just as game as he was to spend months experimenting, reading, and talking about food. There was no relationship between the time expended to put on these dinners and the prices charged—they were a labor of love rather than a quest for profit. According to Escalona's recollection, the day after photos of one of their meals were posted on Instagram, Lalo began to criticize his technique as he removed the fat from a braise, telling Escalona that before he played at being a chef, he needed to learn the work of being in the kitchen. "If you started to commit a series of errors, he began to have an attitude toward you like, 'I guess you need to learn this the hard way.' He can be childish in the way he handles things in the kitchen and it creates a lot of conflict. You either admire him so much that you don't want to disappoint him, or it turns out he isn't who you thought, and then you leave. I would have loved to have stayed longer and learned more, but it was very difficult. I didn't see him as a leader, just a boss. And I came looking for a leader."

For weeks, Escalona debated whether to quit. When he finally told Lalo he was leaving to work on his own project, Lalo told him he was welcome to come back whenever he wanted.

After he left, even as Escalona developed the Sexto Colectivo and found work at a Japanese restaurant, he remained obsessed with the goings-on at Máximo and frequently checked in with his ex-coworkers. Among them were long-term employees, people who had earned Lalo's admiration over years. They included Mariana Alfarache, who had been made head chef of Lalo!; Andrés Trujillo, who was eventually promoted to chef de partie at Máximo; Alejandro Gil, the sous-chef at Máximo; Gerardo Ramos, the chef de cuisine at Havre 77; and Oscar Luna Rivera, the longtime manager of Máximo. Ending his time at Máximo was painful for Escalona. He wanted to stay; he wanted to leave. "It was a blow to the ego—to realize that I'm one of the people who couldn't handle him." He came to peace with the decision. In time, his fixation with the goings-on of the kitchen abated as his own projects gained momentum, but he continued to study the food, as a customer.

————

Andrés Trujillo grew up in Venezuela and began his restaurant career at Alto, the top fine dining restaurant in Caracas. It was frequently shuttered due to chaotic protests and insecurity. For a young cook, fundamental lessons were being missed, while other, crueler ones were learned. For years, you could find foie gras and extra virgin olive oil in the city's boutique shops, while the foundation of the Venezuelan diet—*harina pan* and oil for making *arepas*—were scarce. Sometimes, Trujillo and his fellow cooks would prepare food all day for the tasting menu at Alto and then a protest would strike. They'd have to cancel reservations as the streets filled with tear gas and barricades were set aflame. Huddled inside, they'd eat the food themselves.

When another chef left Máximo, Trujillo was promoted. At first, he fell a few steps behind, unable to anticipate Lalo's next move, and became the subject of Lalo's constant frustration. He observed Lalo's critiques from an emotional remove. In the moment it could be intense, sure, but when he forced himself to focus on the content of what Lalo was saying instead of getting caught up in the emotion of being criticized, he found it was usually valid. He'd stop, breathe, try again. When he got frustrated, it was with the other cooks in the kitchen who seemed to be less invested. Weren't they here to be the best?

Trujillo drew a distinction between cooks and chefs. In his eyes, Lalo was worth following because he managed to be both. Like Scott Adair, the Atlanta cook who became Lalo's first fan, Trujillo watched Lalo's hands. As they added a few flakes of salt to finish a dish. As they caressed a shipment of truffles. As they clenched a piece of brioche and assessed the speed at which it rebounded. "We say, *cuando un chef tiene mano*," he explained—literally, "when a chef has the hand" for cooking. Lalo could touch a piece of fruit and determine whether it had reached peak ripeness, he could sense the imbalance of flavor on a plated dish by the too-heavy dollop of sauce that had left his spoon. Those skills translated beyond efficiency; such a chef could call on an inspiring image, a song lyric, a feeling, then create an edible manifestation. A bright, faintly sweet scallop ceviche tasted of a tangerine sunset over the Pacific at Verana. A childhood memory of the Estado de México brought the humble black bean into conversation with chocolate clams and the peppery petals of shaved radish. Many of his dishes—red mole with octopus, beans, green apple, and cilantro—seemed utterly original. That was only an illusion; some cook, somewhere, had combined the elements before, but this particular assembly was distinctly Lalo's. The green apple was sliced thin and plated sparingly, a tart note that played on the herbs in the mole. His selection of the best-quality octopus, the slight char from the grill, the right portion, all of these were part of what Trujillo called Lalo's hand—not only his skill, not only his understanding of flavor, not only his way with presentation, not only his personal experiences and the way they inspired his cooking. It was all of these working in concert. As Trujillo improved, Lalo paid for him to travel to England to stage at other restaurants. He was promoted to chef de partie, in charge of hot dishes, including sauces, proteins, and garnishes. They developed a friendship.

———

Gabriel Rodríguez, the first sous-chef that Lalo hired, stayed at Máximo Bistrot for nearly four years. He had talent and passion, a work ethic that you couldn't fake. He was fast and nimble, and the two men seemed to find a quick, balletic rhythm in the small kitchen. Gabriel was motivated rather than intimidated by Lalo, like a ferociously competitive teammate.

Gabriel grew up in Iztapalapa, a large borough—1.8 million strong—of Mexico City, where some of the capital's endemic problems are made most glaring: it claims some of the highest rates of rape and domestic violence in a country battling with the phenomenon of femicide (the murder of a woman motivated by gender), and pollution exacerbated by an inadequate water supply, with scores of diesel-powered trucks heaving up its hills to fill residents' cisterns every day.

Gabriel was eighteen, still finishing his technical diploma in gastronomy as a high school student, when he got his first job at Pujol in 2010. He made the hours-long commute from Iztapalapa to Polanco on a series of buses.

"I didn't even realize what Pujol was. I saw it written up in a magazine, but what I took from that article was, 'OK, here's a person who is making his own way,'" he said of Olvera. Gabriel had spent a few days auditioning to be hired as a cook at Pujol when he got a bad case of indigestion; in a panic, he told Lalo, then the restaurant's chef de cuisine, that he had to leave early. The next day, the sous-chef was enraged; Gabriel had informed Lalo that he was leaving, but not his direct superior. The punishment for that offense happened to coincide with the resignation of two dishwashers, who were replaced by Gabriel alone. He figured he would be trapped behind the sink for a day. That day turned into weeks. He was offered a position to stay on—as the sole dishwasher. Still, his post behind the sink afforded him a full view of Mexico's premier kitchen, and he decided to stay. "It was a starting point."

The only way to be noticed was with good work. Gabriel would get into a trance state, churning through the stack of dishes like he was leveling up in a video game. As soon as he had sprayed and scrubbed away the charred contents of one pan, another showed up in its place. His turn as dishwasher lasted three months before he was invited to cook again. Then he worked garnishes and made the restaurant's tortillas, a high-pressure job: many of the restaurant's other dishes would be elevated or marred depending on his ability. Within a year of being hired, he was promoted to chef de partie, in charge of all the appetizers that left the kitchen—including the tortilla soup, the *huarache de wagyu*, the shrimp flauta, and the Veracruz-style ceviche. When others doubted Gabriel, Lalo told them to hold their tongue. "I fell in love with him," says Gabriel, "because I thought, 'Wow, he believes in me!'"

The short story of why Gabriel left Pujol is that he had a love affair with a fellow cook who was already in a relationship with yet another member of the staff. He left heartbroken. When he resigned, he provided no explanation, in order to spare his former lover a scandal. "You'll be here until when?" his boss asked. "Right now," Gabriel said. "I'm leaving." The exit was shocking. Gabriel had decided to leave the top restaurant in the country, where his talent had been recognized and promoted in spite of his age; not only was he abandoning the best job he was likely to be offered, but doing so unsure if he could count on a recommendation. "I said to myself, 'No, what have I done?'" He was filled with regret, but he never considered returning. After that, he spent a few months working at restaurants in Chiapas and Veracruz. By then, Lalo and Gaby were ready to open Máximo Bistrot and hired him.

Gabriel was of a new generation in Mexico's kitchens: he was becoming a world-class professional in restaurants his countrymen had created. He didn't need to stage abroad, much less make risky border crossings to do so. He could grow and flourish at home.

To Gabriel that was possible because of the nature of the work. "It's work you do with your hands. Anyone can develop their talent and focus it and create so much more out of that, regardless of where they come from." He made the ascent look easy, but that magic combination of talent and drive was hard to find. Some cooks had tons of ambition but their aspirations gave them tunnel vision, and they failed to work as members of a team. Others were collaborative but lacked the drive that might push them up the ranks. Still others had a strong work ethic and plenty of talent but lived far away and were constantly late—a problem that reflected only the basic principles of geography and the failings of the city's transportation system, but resulted in castigation at work. And still others were hardworking, local, ambitious, and talented, but were disorganized, contaminating the work of everyone in their orbit. They'd finish a task to perfection, then leave behind a dirty rag and a messy table that quickly led to chaos in a kitchen's cramped quarters.

Gabriel's relationship with Lalo came with its own bitter pills. On one occasion, a few years after he began at Máximo, a series of misunderstandings over the course of a shift led to one of Lalo's most spectacular breakdowns on record. Gabriel had been doing prep work in the small room above the kitchen when another cook placed a tray of ravioli haphazardly on the edge of a rack. Gabriel bumped into the tray and sent the ravioli raining down on the floor. He picked them up and put them in the trash and then set about making a new tray to compensate. He was having a good day, his work humming along at a clip, and the extra task didn't set him back too far. But in the game of telephone that is sometimes played in a restaurant kitchen, a mangled message got back to Lalo: that Gabriel had knocked over and picked up the ravioli, and then placed them right back on the tray awaiting service.

Lalo was livid. To make an example, he threw food on the floor, one piece after another, with the other cooks standing around as the dumbstruck audience. "Would you serve *this* to a customer?" Splat! "How about *this*?" In Gabriel's memory, the tirade lasted for fifteen minutes, an eternity in the life of the kitchen, and hundreds of examples covered the floor. When it ended, he walked through the mess and out the service door. It wouldn't be the first or last time Lalo left the kitchen stunned with a tirade, a hurled object or expletive.

When Lalo and Gabriel reconciled a year later and Gabriel had returned to Máximo, Lalo suggested him as a competitor on Mexico's second season of *Top Chef*, despite the fact that this would require three paid months off. He went on to win the competition and $100,000. After the television stint ended, Lalo balked at what he saw as a marked change in Gabriel's attitude: his humble mentee had been transformed into a minor celebrity who didn't really need the job anyway—he had not only cash to spare, but plenty of other job offers. One day, Gabriel, on his way to attend an awards ceremony, told Lalo he wanted to take two days off of work instead of one—he planned to properly celebrate his win with the party of his life, which would require a day of recovery. To Lalo, this was the last straw. Though they'd later repair their friendship, Gabriel's time at Máximo was over: Lalo fired Gabriel, who hadn't planned to return.

Though Lalo had come up in the business during a time when food being thrown at cooks and arguments turning physical were regarded as typical features of kitchen life, he was regretful about his role when asked about some of the clashes in his own kitchen. At the same time, he could be skeptical of critiques from people who hadn't made careers inside professional kitchens. This was an industry that had been built on hierarchy, in a fast-paced, high-stress environment. Each day brought new frustrations: Cooks made each other look bad on purpose. They defied his instructions. They pretended they'd finished work they hadn't started and lied to cover up mistakes in the work they had finished. After they left and opened their own restaurants, they served copies of his recipes.

———

Lalo was more cook than entrepreneur. He was often approached with proposals for collaborations, but looked at them tentatively. There were a few exceptions. In 2013, British restaurateur Tarun Mahrotri traveled to Mexico City and came to dine at Máximo. He was on the verge of opening a Mexican restaurant in London called Peyote, and he had come to Mexico City in search of a new cook. He showed up at Máximo again and again, trying to persuade Lalo to join the project. Coincidentally, Lalo had a London vacation planned—he was going to propose to Gaby. Instead, he spent most of the trip in the kitchen of Peyote, working to turn it around before the opening. After Lalo returned (and proposed to Gaby in their apartment), Peyote flickered in the distant background. Being attached to a posh London restaurant was an impressive credit on his résumé and a chance to give some of his cooks the opportunity to work abroad by connecting them to Mahrotri for elusive work visas, but Lalo was not invested in the project, personally or economically.

In 2017, Lalo was invited by Mahrotri to visit what would be Peyote's newest location, in Dubai. This time, Lalo looked at the trip as a chance to finally get some rest. Between sessions with the cooks, he ate long meals, watched movies, and visited the spice souk. One night, he invited a new arrival, Francisco Omaña, to see the Dubai Mall. He needed a gift for Gaby before he headed home, and he loved seeing the expression on people's faces when they glimpsed the mall for the first time. There was a full-size dinosaur skeleton, a three-story aquarium with sharks, and branches of restaurants from all over the world. Omaña, also from Mexico, had been compelled to come to Dubai from Peyote's London location after he was unable to renew his British visa.

The mall's entrances were each equipped with detailed maps that laid out the sections of the mammoth building. Lalo zeroed in on one called Fashion Avenue, and walked toward Gucci. He looked over the jackets, then headed for a pair of silver loafers—Gaby had had her eye on the shoes in gold, but the store was out of stock. Lalo snapped a picture and texted it to Gaby. She answered: three smiling emojis with hearts for eyes. Lalo had lost his credit card early in the trip ("I'm so fucking dependent for everything, I can't do shit alone"), and one of the investors in Peyote had given him the equivalent of a few thousand dollars in dirhams, part of his payment, which he carried around loose in the pocket of his shorts.

The saleswoman retrieved the pair of shoes unceremoniously from the stockroom. Omaña noted the price tag on a jacket—1,500 euro—and began backing away from the racks of merchandise, eyeing them as if they might shatter upon contact. He ended up somewhere in the center of the store, a few safe feet away with his arms crossed in front of his chest, while Lalo paid and was handed the shopping bag. The ambiance inside the store was aloof; people made purchases, parting from huge sums, and walked uneventfully back into the corridors of commerce.

By that point, Lalo had been in Dubai for a few weeks, at the beach house where Mahrotri was staying. He was uncharacteristically well-rested, having gotten nine or ten hours of sleep most nights. When he woke up, he'd breakfast on whatever had been brought in: fresh pomegranate juice, pulpy and light, or full-fat organic yogurt imported from England, thick and tasting of sunshine. In the quiet mornings he'd sit on a patio chair, facing the calm, gray waters of the Persian Gulf. He absentmindedly scanned through his iPhone, checking the news and images on Instagram that had gone up in Mexico while he was sleeping. The house was part of the Palm Jumeirah complex, one of the world's most ostentatious displays of wealth: a man-made, palm tree-shaped peninsula. The central trunk juts out from mainland Dubai, crowded with high-rise apartment buildings and luxury malls. Extending from the trunk, islands shaped like skinny fronds fan into the ocean, with orderly lines of homes; owners can enjoy early morning swims at a beach house that's just a thirty-minute drive from the office. Circling the palm is a crescent of land where hotels and a water park draw tourists. Viewed via satellite, you can also see a second palm that's nearly identical, the development of which was suspended during the 2008 financial crisis. They are startling decorative addendums to the Earth's geography: humanity, unsatisfied with the majesty of the natural world, decided to make a few "improvements."

From Lalo's vantage point, with his feet propped on a generic beige patio table, surrounded by ever-green Astroturf and a line of cheap tiki torches, the landscape didn't seem particularly dramatic. The sky was hazy and the water didn't sparkle.

Over the past five years, he and Gaby had fine-tuned and expanded their businesses and were enjoying their success, but they were still trying to determine how far to scale up. Peyote felt like an exploratory step into an international restaurant scene where Lalo's contemporaries, like Olvera (who had opened the acclaimed Cosme in New York in 2014) and Gabriela Cámara (of Contramar and its San Francisco cousin, Cala, circa 2015), had recently found an audience. Lalo, barred from entering the U.S., would have to look for other possibilities. He couldn't so much as visit the restaurants he heard about in New York, Portland, or San Francisco. Instead, he traveled within Mexico and, when time allowed, to Tokyo, Copenhagen, Paris, Madrid, Palermo.

When it came down to it, Lalo wasn't getting paid all that much to help with Peyote's menu, and he hadn't been given a percentage of the businesses or any formal stake. He wasn't sure he wanted one—after he and Gaby had carefully built their businesses in Mexico, being involved in every last detail, he was ambivalent about deepening his connection to restaurants founded on someone else's vision, too far away for him to verify the quality day-to-day. Still, the trip afforded him a break from his punishing routine in the kitchen. In his daily life in Mexico City, he never had time to sleep a full night, much less to sit and think. He usually arrived at Máximo before 7 a.m., took a break between 4 and 6 p.m., and then worked until midnight. He rarely took a full day off. The five or six hours he worked each day training the staff in Dubai to cook from his menu felt like nothing compared to his usual marathon days, sweating every last detail. He hadn't learned as much from the project of opening Peyote, he said, as he had "from not having so much shit in my head."

Lalo found Dubai itself unattractive and soulless, but, coming

from a country where corruption undercut authority, he was fascinated by its encyclopedia of idiosyncratic rules: swearing in public
was illegal; you couldn't buy booze at a liquor store without a special
permit, but you could drink at a bar or restaurant; jaywalking was
actively fined. Lalo's skepticism of Dubai combined with his intense
interest in its norms gave the trip the quality of study abroad.

Mostly, he watched how the migrants were treated.

"It's crazy. Crazy. The moment they don't need them here,
everybody's gone. When they finish the construction of this place
and there's no more jobs, everybody's gone. They get paid so little.
They don't have enough money to go to places like this," Lalo said,
gesturing at the dining room of Le Petit Maison. But the potential
for upward mobility impressed him. "The idea is to beat everyone
around you. There's so much happening that you can become a general manager within a year—*if* you move, *if* you work."

Mid-morning, the international group of young cooks who had
been recruited to Peyote arrived at the house by van and began testing recipes. Pork was off-limits, which meant no *cochinita*, *chicharron*,
carnitas, *frijoles a la charra*, or *al pastor*. Instead, they worked on a
ceviche of mild white fish in coconut milk infused with vanilla bean,
and a shrimp aguachile topped with slices of chile serrano. They
made a jicama, pinto bean, and cilantro salad, and tested batches of
churros, each time calculating small adjustments to the batter and
timing. After the cooks set up, Lalo bounded into the kitchen like a
coach heading into a Little League dugout. Here, he was unburdened
by the daily dramas that molded his demeanor in his own restaurants. His task was to impart a fundamental understanding of Mexican food to the cooks from India, Nepal, and the Philippines, and to
encourage the few Mexican cooks to become leaders in the kitchen
after he departed, but he had nothing at stake.

While Lalo had never visited the countries Peyote's cooks hailed from, he understood what it was like to live outside his own country, laboring to prepare food for clients who wouldn't have met his eyes if they passed him in the street. When he was their age, he, too, was cooking dishes with flavor profiles that were utterly foreign to him. In the process, he developed a worldly palate and learned to see the connections between seemingly distinct cuisines. A Nepalese chef could prepare a ceviche that would please any Mexican, even riff on a core concept, once he learned the principles of the dish.

"If you go to Paris, all of the cooks in the old bistros are Bangladeshi, even the famous ones—they're like the Mexican cooks in New York who cook all the best pasta at Lilia's."

The cooks were staying in housing guaranteed by their visas, on the edge of the emirate. They couldn't walk far—certainly not to the Palm Jumeirah or to Peyote's location in the Dubai International Financial Center, next to the Four Seasons Hotel. They were driven to and from their obligations by van, so any recreation had to be carefully coordinated with the end of a shift, otherwise they'd have to make the long commute home on public transit or pay an exorbitant price for a cab. Some days the sky was heavy and opaque, but rather than the pollution that could slather the atmosphere in Mexico City a sickly gray, the air here was gritty with sandstorms. They were, after all, in the middle of the desert, in a Las Vegas-like playground for the rich that had sprung up with stunning speed after the discovery of oil in the 1960s. The skyline was filled with cranes and expansion seemed to only be speeding up.

For wealthy international tourists, there was more than enough to do. They could walk underwater wearing a scuba mask, skydive over the palms, parasail, ski down snow-covered slopes at an indoor resort, then ride through the red dunes on camelback. They could party at restaurants like Peyote, which competed for their euros and dollars and dirhams. A handful of Peyote's staff could afford to dabble in these luxurious pastimes, but others had taken the job and traveled far from home so they could send back every spare penny to their families. Some cooks used as little as possible of their living stipend to pay rent in housing shared with a dozen other workers. Like Lupe, they spent what they saved on the construction of houses back in the countries they hoped to return to one day.

After recipe testing, Lalo and the cooks hopped into the company van and headed to the shell of the new restaurant. For now, it was a box of high-end real estate filled with activity: a construction crew that hailed primarily from India and the Philippines were busy painting walls, installing lights, and intercepting furniture from Mexico. The floors were coated in dust and splintered wood. There were no tables or chairs. The cooks sat on the ground and leaned against the walls, chatting in English and Spanish as they checked Facebook and WhatsApp. They wandered the crypt-like kitchen underneath the restaurant, which had previously housed Wheeler's of St. James's, by famed British chef Marco Pierre White. Then, they discussed what to eat and where. They couldn't afford the perfect specimens of sushi at Zuma or the crab and lobster salad at Le Petit Maison. But outside of the immediate courtyard they could find chana masala, panang curry, lamb kofta, gruyère crepes, soup dumplings. Omaña discovered how other cultures took a familiar ingredient like garbanzo beans, then infused them with layers of spices that emerged and subsided on the palate, leaving you with a memory that lingered for days.

The restaurant's staff hailed from twenty-seven countries, including the Philippines, Spain, Poland, Serbia, India, Jamaica, Colombia, Portugal, Ukraine, Nepal, and, of course, Mexico. A few days before Peyote was set to open, Mahrotri flew in his guru, Jag-

dish Prasad Sharma, from India, to lead a ceremony to bless the staff
and the space. On the day of the fire ritual, which Sharma performed
to energize the staff, prevent accidents, and ensure the food tasted
good to customers, the atmosphere was electric. Whereas the previous week, Peyote had been a messy lair of nails and wet paint, today it
was filled with comfortable armchairs upholstered in sea-foam green
fabric, handmade wood and marble tables, and Oaxacan tilework.
The paint had mostly dried and the lighting was soft and gold-tinted.
The staff gathered in the kitchen, and each person had a red *tilak*
painted on their forehead, suppressing giddy energy as they waited
for Sharma to pray. Sharma, in turn, waited for Mahrotri to get off
his cell phone, while Mahrotri waited to talk to a customer service
representative from his credit card company. Afterward, they sat in a
circle in the dining room as the ritual took place.

The cooks had been brought here for their skills and their willingness to leave their families to put their labor into something that
might yield a modest return, while investors anticipated a massive
one. There was immense pressure to perform. Millions of dollars had
been poured into the restaurant's renovation before it even opened
its doors—but the cooks barely had a chance to practice in the professional kitchen before they welcomed paying customers.

Serving Mexican food in one of the world's most expensive pieces
of real estate was a daring business decision. There were only a handful of fine dining Mexican restaurants in the world outside of Mexico;
cultivating a willingness in the clientele to pay what they'd readily
dole out for Japanese or French cuisine would require a paradigm
shift. What's more, alcohol sales would be modest, since many of the
clients would be observant Muslims. With so many profits in the London location coming from margaritas and mezcal, the concern was
significant.

Lalo sat the cooks down around a marble table in a corner of the restaurant's dining room. He talked quietly and they leaned toward him to listen above the din.

"If you want something, you can have it—*if* you work for it," he said. "People are not just going to give you something. People are not going to take care of you. You have to work for it. There's a difference between my country and this country that I learned when I first came here, and people have told me this five times already: 'In Dubai, if you work hard, you can climb up really fast because the workforce is needed. Everything here is about the workforce.' In my country, sometimes guys—cooks or waiters—have been doing it for fifteen years, and they're still waiters. Fifteen years. If you don't work for it, it's because you don't want it. You're not happy because you're not getting things your way? You know? You have to work for it. If you want people to treat you with respect, what do you do? You treat them with—"

"Respect," they chimed in.

"If you want to be happy," Lalo continued, "you have to ask yourself what makes you happy and put yourself in that situation. You know? When I travel to other countries and they ask me where I'm from and I say, 'I'm from Mexico,' they always say, 'Oh, *burro!*' They think in Mexico we are so far behind, like we ride donkeys. They always think of the sombrero and the mustache, and you know, they always think of a violent country and always think of drugs. In reality, it's a country like every other country in the world. It could be a superpower; it's a country with very intelligent people. It's a country *with* drugs. It's a country *with* donkeys. It's a country *with* people with mustaches. They never think about us as anything other than ignorant people, an ignorant person riding a donkey or wearing a sombrero, you know?"

Lalo hadn't planned on giving this speech, but whether he was talking to the waiters about a new dish before service or to a customer about global warming, speeches spilled easily from his lips. Maybe it would be meaningless to these listeners and maybe, alone and uncertain about the future, it was just the show of solidarity they were hungry for—to hear that even this famous chef who had been flown across the world to teach them understood what it was to be dismissed and overlooked. To feel underestimated.

Then, as if in response to this narrow-minded idea of his country, Lalo began to explain its regional nuances. How in northern Mexico, they raise cattle and eat big cuts of steak, but how their diet is limited by the fickle land. How this cuisine, which lacks the diversity of ingredients available in the south, is also one of the best known north of the border with the United States. But even the food in the north inspired Lalo—the chiles, cooked whole, the use of soy sauce brought by Chinese immigrants. The refashioning of a used plow disc into a wok-shaped cooking surface—a *discada*. At Máximo, he explained, he made *chiles toreados* with a vinaigrette, tucked them into a slice of seared duck breast or the trimmings from a filet mignon and gave them to the customers for free.

————

Over the coming months, the cohort of Mexican cooks struggled to adjust to Dubai. The clients, they found, were quite a bit different from the ones back home: they ordered excessive amounts of food, took photos, and often left the plates untouched. A friend told Omaña about an incredible cup of coffee he'd had at a hotel restaurant. What made it so good?, Omaña asked. It was flaked with gold. The emirate, he began to feel, was designed for the age of social media, when posting something flashy was currency, regardless of the quality of the experience in real life. The city was intolerant, and Omaña wasn't happy with the job or the heat. He lived for his time off and spent his savings on trips to Southeast Asia. On his final trip from Dubai he flew to the Philippines, then took a plane, then a bus, then a Jeep, then walked an hour into the jungle. He picked a banana from a tree, peeled off the thin yellow skin, and took a bite. It was starchy and sweet. He thought about the bananas he'd eaten in Dubai but couldn't summon the flavor. *That place is going to eat up my life,* Omaña thought. The restaurant folded almost as soon as he left.

Once Lalo had taught the cooks the menu, his work was done. He had his own restaurants and employees to get back to. He had Gaby to get back to. The day before Peyote opened its doors, he boarded a plane, rested and ready to return to work. He picked up another pair of loafers at Gucci during his stopover in London Heathrow, this time in gold.

CHAPTER TEN

HOME

NATALIA FLEW TO Mexico on one of her routine visits. She longed to go to her house in the Estado de México, to sleep in the bed she'd shared with Lupe so long ago, but she had other places to visit first. She began at Lalo and Gaby's apartment in the Colonia Roma and cooked Lalo's favorite foods so they could eat together when he ducked out of the kitchen for a late lunch. Then, she went to San José de las Pilas, in time for the annual celebration of the village's namesake saint. While most of her siblings were now living in Atlanta, a few of them also made the pilgrimage for the festival. Migration had left the town quiet and a bit eerie, full of empty homes like the ones her siblings had built with plans of eventual retirement. Each March, San José de las Pilas seemed to quadruple in population, and the visitors were obvious from their new clothes and cell phones.

Natalia and her siblings walked through the cobblestone streets, following a procession for San José, carrying umbrellas to protect them from the intense sun as they stepped around piles of manure. Devotees carried an altar with a statue of the saint, decorated with hundreds of fresh flowers. At each house, the procession stopped and women dropped confetti on top of San José's head, which fell down his bearded cheeks and yellow robe to rest at his feet. A burst of fireworks went off at close range, and the children covered their ears and waited a half block away until it was safe to continue on.

They cooked *arrachera* tacos at Natalia's sister Juana's house. She had the most acreage, and they looked out toward the mountains as they browned the meat on a comal that had been fashioned from an old plow disc, the method Lalo had recounted to the cooks in Dubai. Her brother Pedro, who still lived in the village, had raised the cow for the beef, and grown the tomatoes, onions, garlic, and chile for the salsa, which they blackened before tossing into a blender with salt: salsa tatemada. They sat around eating while the kids ran across a clearing that framed a view of mountains and a lake in the distance.

Lupe was never far from Natalia's thoughts, and as she followed the procession through the hot streets, her memories took hold. He'd been a dedicated Catholic and had taken on the considerable task of fundraising for the festival. It was here in the simple church in the center of the village that friends and strangers had been by her side to mourn his passing, and then had gathered in the adjacent houses to serve mole, chicken, and rice. At the crest of a small hill above the main plaza, Natalia peered into the shallow stone well where she'd spent every day of her childhood hauling buckets of water for bathing, cleaning and cooking. The water was green-blue and clear, and she could see tadpoles wriggling at the bottom. She'd labored here, under a grand mesquite tree with her sisters, washing her family's clothes and rags in the consolation of its shade, while her neighbors brought their horses to drink at the stone troughs a few yards away.

By the time Natalia left the village, she had four children and was raising them almost entirely alone. She was twenty-three.

Decades later, when she thought back to San José de las Pilas, she remembered the hardships, the rules in her father's house. But now, relaxing in Juana's yard surrounded by her family, drinking cold beer in the sunshine, eating, laughing at one of her siblings' stories or just sitting quietly in their company, she couldn't decide if she longed for her youth.

Earlier that day, she had wandered around her childhood home with her brother Martin, admiring the work they'd put into fixing up the second floor of what was now a brick and concrete building. When she was growing up, the walls were made of adobe bricks and the floor of dried clay. In the yard, she pointed out the worn-down metate where she'd spent hours doubled over, grinding corn kernels for masa and the seeds that went into various moles.

Through Martin's gaze, the memories refracted in a different direction.

"It was lovely, because we grew up free, remember?" Martin said. "We were in the streets, running around. When we finished work in the afternoons we went out to play with the other children. There was poverty, but we were so happy."

In the mornings, they had fetched eggs from their chickens and cracked them open on the hot comal, while their mother pounded salsa in the molcajete. Natalia found herself agreeing with her brother. "*Eramos bien felices*," she said, with an inward-facing smile. We were really happy. The food was nutritious, there were no chemicals. They ate *verduras criollas*, the vegetables indigenous to this land, including tomatoes, beans, and corn in every shade of red, purple, and gold.

This was the place Lalo had come from. It was the place he was always trying to return to. When he served beans at Máximo—an ingredient he celebrated as the essence of campesino food—it was a gesture toward his origins. But how to return? He framed his identity around this collection of houses and fields in the mountains. "*Quieren ver mi ranchito?*" he'd ask the waiters. You want to see my village? They did. He'd Google photos of the town and pass around his phone. When he got overwhelmed by stress, he and Gaby sometimes hopped on a flight to France or Italy. Sometimes they took Natalia along. There they would visit the cutting-edge restaurants and the traditional bistros, and Lalo looked for inspiration and a way to clear his head. But after a couple of weeks, what began as an amazing, incredible, enviable respite turned garish and empty. Lalo felt the extra pounds around his middle and came home to a diet of papaya and cucumber. He could always return to the village, and he did so often in his mind. It grounded him. But when he managed to return in person, to leave flowers on Lupe's grave or see his grandparents' house, he felt unsettled, out of place. People knew his family, but he hadn't lived there since he was two years old. He worried about how he might be perceived, in his new car, stopping by to talk to whom and see what, exactly? The shell of the house where he'd lived as a baby?

Natalia knew how to return. The question was, how to remember? Her memories shifted in ways that unsteadied her and she grew dubious of her hold on them. The village was hers, but she didn't have a home here anymore. Had Lupe been alive during the past decade, he might have spent it building a place for them to come back to one day, as her siblings had done. As it stood, the only home left for Natalia in her country of origin was the one they'd made in the Estado de México.

After they'd eaten, the family walked to the rodeo ground. A full band, fifteen members deep, took the stage wearing matching red blazers. They swayed back and forth to the drumbeat, while down in the ring, a skinny cowboy—*un jinete*—dried the sweat from his palms with the dusty earth and prepared to mount an aging bull that was ushered into a pen with a rope around its testicles. Announcers tried to whip up excitement in the crowd,

"*Listo! Listo! Listo! Listo! Listo! Listo! Listo! Listoooo! Echale Soña-dor de Morelia! Lo hemos decidido, el jinete se dispone a jugarse la vida!*" Ready! Ready! Ready! Ready! Ready! Ready! Ready! Readyyyyyy! Go for it, Dreamer from Morelia! We're decided: the rider is ready to play with his life!

The bull had just one horn, and though it bucked when the rope was tightened, it was too tired to unseat the Dreamer from Morelia. Vendors hawked plastic cups of pink watermelon juice, bright green piles of steamed garbanzo beans still in their shells, and the boiled peanuts that so many had grown accustomed to snacking on in Georgia and Texas. Everything was served with Valentina hot sauce, *chamoy*—a sweet-sour condiment made with fruit, chile powder, and sugar—and slices of lime. Like her neighbors, Natalia had freshened up before the rodeo and put on sharp new clothes. The men wore gleaming cowboy boots and white Tejano hats. A few napped on their wives' shoulders after a long day of celebrating. The sun began its descent until everything glowed.

It was the end of the dry season, and in the pastures around the town, the chlorophyll had been baked out of the grass, turning it the color of wheat. Natalia walked with her family to the square in front of the church to dance and watch the fireworks display, an epic spectacle that threatened to burn the village to ash. In the morning, she boarded a bus back to Mexico City. She longed for her house, the place she and Lupe and the children had built with their hands, the place that always put her at peace.

The next day, Lalo and Gaby drove her to the Estado de México. Natalia got out of the car in the narrow alleyway and opened the black metal gate. On her last visit, she had walked through the same gate and seen the squat, moss-green home that she'd built with Lupe's remittances, the poinsettias in the circle of soil in the center of a concrete courtyard, the rebar reaching skyward. Today, she saw a modern white building with clean lines, wood and stone accents, wide picture windows, and a line of cacti in terra-cotta pots on the roof. Lalo had taken the bones of the home she'd built with Lupe, saving just the walls of the first few rooms and tearing down the other structures. He'd outfitted the house with a marble bathroom and new floors, a rooftop patio with a glass enclosure, a modern kitchen. It could easily have been in an upscale section of Los Angeles or Miami. The façade was hidden away from the street, obscured from prying eyes.

For less than five minutes, Natalia stood at the entrance, taking it in. If anger flashed through her, it was quickly displaced by a protracted sadness. She got back in the car. When her daughters asked her what the new house was like, she couldn't recollect any of the details. All she knew was that it wasn't her house.

Lalo was disappointed by his mother's reaction, but Gaby told him to be patient. To give Natalia time to get used to it. "What didn't you like?" he asked. "I don't know, I don't remember it!" she told him.

A few months later, Natalia came back to Mexico, anxious to see the house again. She sat in the back seat, and Lalo turned on a talk radio station as they made the congested drive, less than twenty miles but more than an hour from the city on a Monday morning. The host discussed mounting insecurity in the country's capital. As the government's ill-fated war against the drug cartels had raged over the past decade, Mexico City had been considered relatively safe. But at the end of 2018, when Andrés Manuel López Obrador took the presidency, the city was closing in on its most violent year on record. If crime in Mexico City was on the rise, crime in the Estado de México was far worse. There, grisly murders of women, their remains tossed into rank sewage canals, had become commonplace. In 2019, 8,345 people disappeared in Mexico.

Gaby, Lalo, and Natalia arrived at the house. This time, Natalia slowly made her way around the property, stopping to admire the renovation from different angles. She took in the lawn and the citrus trees that had been planted since her last visit, and noted the places where the new tile needed fixing. Her particleboard furniture from the 1980s had been revarnished. She wasn't coming back to her house, but she had arrived at a very beautiful house, she decided. Maybe when she took her things out of the boxes and put photos on the walls, it would begin to feel like home. As a renewed sense of peace began to settle, Lalo barreled into the yard, a ball of anxiety.

"You can't go out around here. You can't leave. You can't go out in the street," Lalo told Natalia.

"Why?"

"Didn't you listen to everything we were listening to on the way in?"

"I was listening, but over here, too?"

"It's even worse here," Lalo said.

When he and Gaby left, Natalia started to go through boxes and suitcases that had been stored in the new shower. Before construction, Lalo had tossed anything that was decidedly broken, but he'd kept the odds and ends for her to sort through. She spread the items out on the bed and the floor: a pair of sweatpants with a patched knee; print-outs of recipes that Lalo had made when he was working at Van Gogh's; a tattered copy of Anthony Bourdain's *Kitchen Confidential*; a grammar-school project of Maria's depicting the location of glands in the male and female anatomy with peppermints, which

Lalo had picked off and eaten; a dark green bottle of Polo by Ralph Lauren with a gold top—Lupe's favorite cologne.

Natalia wiped the dust off of an old picture frame that held an image of swans floating in a lake, with a clock in the corner that had been stuck at 3:35 for who knew how many years. She remembered making payments to buy the clock on layaway. It had cost 25 pesos. Wait, she thought, that didn't seem right. Maybe it had cost 200 pesos.

The contractor, Manolo, stuck around to help Natalia. The builders of the original house, like the others around it, were self-taught, Manolo said. They had used decent materials but didn't know quite what they were doing. "We just wanted to have a roof!" Natalia told him. They'd eaten rice, beans, and nopales to save any money they could for the materials to continue construction. "It was a lot of effort. Then you blink, and it's all gone."

But Natalia was eager to make this house a home. She wanted Manolo to get the water running and the gas connected so she could come back and spend the night. "I don't want to remember things from the past. You have to live in the now," Natalia said. "They say you have to distance yourself a little from the memories, no? But that they stay in our hearts?"

CHAPTER ELEVEN

TO GROW RADISHES

LALO AND GABY had spent the last few years in debate: should they contract their businesses, move to the countryside, and start an organic farm that would supply the ingredients for a small restaurant and inn? Or should they expand Máximo, create more jobs, and, in the process, put themselves under more pressure?

October of 2019 found Gaby and Lalo walking through a cavernous, warehouse-style building, avoiding stagnant puddles of water as they surveyed progress on what would soon be their new restaurant. For now, it was just one enormous room, lit by a few bare bulbs. The floor was a mosaic of half-finished surfaces. At the front, slats of wood pressed against the windows to shut out the possibility of rubbernecking, and the sign outside betrayed nothing of what was to come. It resembled a half-finished gymnasium, with a corrugated metal roof pinned by thin beams. Concrete walls were covered with chipping paint that hinted at the space's former incarnations, including an automotive repair shop and a pool hall. In the back, a square of earth was marked out—the future home of a tree that would grow indoors, luxuriating under a skylight.

On this day, the tree and the skylight were just drawings on a set of blueprints. Gaby looked, as usual, composed. But her eyes were tense and withholding. She seemed oblivious to the hammering, the specks of dirt floating through the air, the Spanish rendition of "The Little Drummer Boy" that blared through a set of cheap speakers. Believing this dark, muddy pit would one day become the restaurant of their dreams required a suspension of disbelief.

When Gaby and Lalo had first considered this space, they were quoted what seemed like an exorbitant fee just to have the privilege of becoming renters. But after consulting with other chefs, they came to realize it would be par for the course. Should they do it?

"If you don't, somebody else will," a fellow restaurateur told Gaby.

They were favorable clients compared to other options the land-lord might encounter, investors on the hunt for space in a district that was increasingly known for its nightlife. A dance club or bar could be noisy and attract crime and drugs. Lalo and Gaby were successful, after all, and, God willing, would be there for many years.

De Lisle was still the third member of their team. They met in Paris and ate everywhere they could, getting inspired. The space Lalo and Gaby had found in the Roma was essentially a blank canvas: a café and pool hall that could be gutted and made into whatever they imagined. Despite years of dining around the world, de Lisle said, none of them were sure which direction to go.

They considered three influences. First, the outdoor restaurants like Deckman's, where they spent hours eating grilled meat and oys-ters and drinking wine in the Valle de Guadalupe—Mexico's wine region, on the Baja peninsula. The simple buildings were elevated by the food, the landscaping, and the view, and de Lisle found the patina on the aged cement appealing. Second, they thought of the restaurants they'd visited in Northern Europe, like René Redzepi's Noma: a Danish farmhouse with industrial simplicity. Noma features a stone wall, an open dining room filled with light-toned wood, and plants hanging from the rafters. For such an expensive destination restaurant, the design is surprisingly unfussy. Finally, Olvera's Pujol—an insulated space that envelopes you as you walk in, creating its own little world.

They settled on a design inspired by Lalo's own magical thinking as he stood next to the stove, imagining his village: a farmhouse within a warehouse, within one of the world's biggest cities.

The kitchen at the original Máximo wasn't functional anymore— seven or eight cooks jockeyed for space in a galley that could comfortably accommodate four. The restaurant's menu had evolved to include an ever more complex combination of techniques and flavor profiles from across Mexico and France, in addition to Japan, Italy, Spain, and the U.S. South, and they needed more prep space and better equipment.

When they were first starting out, a few of their rich customers encouraged them to raise the prices and make the restaurant more exclusive. Lalo and Gaby balked. We would never do that, they protested. But as Lalo's menu evolved and with it the cost of ingredients, the prices on the menu slowly crept higher. Now, they had to make a choice. "We either float up the current, or down the current," Lalo said, "and what we need to do now is act like restaurateurs."

"We're just very excited about having a proper restaurant, people to feed," Gaby said. "I tell the managers, all the time people are telling us, 'You're the best restaurant in the city.' But we kind of don't *feel* like the best restaurant in the city, because we know how much struggle we have to deliver the things that we're doing. So, I want them to feel empowered, to say, 'Yes! I work in the best restaurant in the city. We have the equipment, we have all these tools to work with and we are doing it properly.' I think that's what we want. We want to rise to the next level."

Over the past decade, Gaby had watched the ease with which Lalo appeared to move through changes—perhaps not in the midst of the daily grind, but big changes that might overwhelm someone else barely seemed to faze him. When opportunities arose or setbacks frustrated them, he seemed to bob along on the waves, buoyed by some internal lightness. Sometimes he rode higher or lower, but he always floated safely above the surface.

But as she took in the vast, dirty space, Gaby's eyes betrayed her: unlike Lalo, she couldn't maintain an air of indifference. She couldn't switch off fear when faced with a possible failure. At least having him by her side reassured her that failure, even spectacular failure, wouldn't sink them for good. His lightness would carry them during times of chaos, and in moments of calm they'd each take a breath, comfort each other, and move on.

Now, Gaby intuited that a change had come—not just to their own lives, but to the city they called home. The movie *Roma* had recently won three Oscars and a steady stream of good press had boosted tourism. The threatening caricature of Mexico embraced by now-president Trump seemed to have spurred a progressive group of travelers to explore Mexico, in rejection of his doom-and-gloom narrative. Watching these shifts, Gaby realized it was time.

Gaby went on a road trip to Morelos to find the mature live tree that was to be the focal point of the new dining room. Soon, it would be transplanted. The kitchen, which had already been designed, would be installed, and on its own would occupy a footprint equivalent to that of the entire original Máximo. The dining room would be bigger, but only by twenty seats. Rent would be higher, and they'd have air conditioning and state-of-the-art equipment—and that meant the economics of the restaurant had to change. The food had to be still more expensive, and an online reservation would require a mandatory credit card hold to ensure that being fully booked reflected a full coffer. It was a practice already in use at some of the city's other top restaurants. This was the restaurant that Lalo's rich patron had envisioned. It was a restaurant designed to vault them into the country's top echelon, among the world's best. And it was a restaurant most people in the city would never experience.

In the meantime, a bone spur had begun to press painfully on the flesh of Lalo's foot, and, while it wasn't visible from the one-meter radius he lorded over behind Máximo's counter, he limped when he walked the streets. His usual sneakers were replaced by inch-and-a-half thick orthotics.

————

The bone spur was only the latest in a series of health issues that had begun to emerge after September 19, 2017, when an earthquake alarm sounded in the city: *wahw-wahw-wahw . . . alerta sísmica, alerta sísmica . . . wahw-wahw-wahw.* Normally, the alarm afforded a few minutes of warning, but the epicenter was too close and the ground began to shudder as its wail echoed through the streets. When the 7.1 quake reached the muddy earth beneath the neighborhoods of Roma and Condesa the pavement seemed to jump, pushing pedestrians up and then collapsing inward. Thousands were injured and more than 200 were killed, hauntingly on the exact same date as the devastating 1985 earthquake. In the weeks and months that followed, residents would learn that the owners of several of the buildings that collapsed had paid off inspectors or skipped construction regulations intended to prevent such tragedies.

After the quake, Lalo's emotional state began to fray. He became convinced that he was suffering from a brain tumor, and traveled to specialists' offices as he sought affirmation of his self-diagnosis and prepared to, consequently, meet his death. He was soon given his answer: anxiety had compounded, and the episodes he'd experienced—nauseous dizzy spells of existential terror—were panic attacks. But he wasn't satisfied and continued to see other doctors, sure that he had a brain tumor or cancer. He lost words, asking for a spoon when he needed a sauté pan, and had trouble pronouncing others. When he went to meet with a neurologist at his tenth-floor office, an acrophobic Lalo had his appointment conducted in the hallway, away from the windows. It barely needed to be said: this search for a succinct, physical explanation for a rapidly tumbling world mimicked Natalia's visits to Florida hospitals, when the doctors had knocked two Tylenol into her palm and sent her back into the wilderness of her life.

When more doctors agreed that he had neither a tumor nor cancer, Lalo blamed the episode on preexisting stress, combined with the two coffees and ginger shake he drank the morning of the earthquake. But he never felt balanced after that. Lalo had recently found his son's photo on Facebook. Max was a teenager now, and he looked like Lalo. His features were more symmetrical, but you could see Lalo in the boy's wide cheekbones and the intensity behind his eyes. When he spoke about his son, Lalo didn't get teary. Wallowing in the loss was too risky. What if he couldn't emerge from the depths? He told Gaby not to let him look at the pictures.

Roma and Condesa were badly hit. Lalo had lived through smaller earthquakes before, and when the ground began to move beneath his feet, he'd expected the impact would be more or less the same: a day without power, a couple of casualties. But as he and Gaby walked the city, taking in the rubble, the people rushing home with tear-stained cheeks, the power lines that hung threateningly in the street, they quickly realized this was different. People spread panicked word of gas leaks, buildings on the verge of collapse, and fires, and it was impossible to discern rumor from fact.

Lalo joined scores of chilangos who set out to feed one another. People circulated with homemade tortas and bottles of water. There were pots of black beans and chicharrones in salsa verde, stacks of pan dulce. Well-resourced restaurants in the most impacted areas, like Contramar in Condesa, served thousands of fish tacos and glasses of *agua de jamaica*. Lalo woke up in the middle of the night to assemble egg, ham, and cheese sandwiches for volunteers, and walked with Gaby at 4 a.m. to collapsed buildings with hot coffee for rescue workers. The neighborhoods would be transformed in the weeks that followed; a local could get lost walking through plazas in the Roma and Condesa that had been tented and repurposed as donation centers, with their own kitchens, sleeping areas, therapists, and, occasionally, masseuses who tried to provide a moment of comfort for families waiting to see if their loved ones would make it out of the rubble alive. Little gestures of solidarity were everywhere, from the free food advertised at cafés to the power strips that neighbors set outside their windows so strangers could recharge their phones.

Seeing this outpouring of care, Lalo balanced hope with cynicism in an interview with *Grub Street*: "Mexicans have always been really kind people, but over the last twenty to thirty years, globalization has changed us. We're not as warm as we used to be. I think we forgot how to be Mexican."

————

While Gaby was searching for the tree in Morelos, a familiar face appeared at the door of Máximo, as familiar faces tended to do: Julio Meléndez, a former cook at the restaurant, stepped haltingly inside. Julio had been working as executive sous-chef at the Hard Rock Hotel on the Riviera Maya when he suffered a stroke and spent thirty-two days in a coma. When he woke up, he had lost mobility on one side of his body but retained his speech, his memories. Julio was still in his late twenties; he had planned to dedicate his life to a career that required intense physicality.

Lalo welcomed Julio and the pair sat down at a table outside. Julio carefully pulled his body—his right side compelling his left—into the chair opposite Lalo.

"I'm recovering," Julio said, determined to get back to his career. "I'll see how I'm able to do it, but I'll do it."

"You have to think about your future," Lalo said, "because—obviously—you're going to do it. You're going to accomplish what you set out to. But of course, you have to think about yourself. You can't just go back and let this happen again."

Lalo recommended that Julio read some books in the meantime, suggestions that originated with Gaby: *Setting the Table* by the hugely successful Shake Shack and Gramercy Tavern owner Danny Meyer, *The Art of the Restaurateur* by Nicholas Lander, and *Kitchen Confidential* by Anthony Bourdain.

Bourdain had committed suicide in 2018, a year before Lalo sat down with Julio. He was Lalo and Gaby's hero. The day they found out he died was among the worst of Lalo's life. Bourdain's death haunted him, a specter of what might come in an industry that could look so appealing from the dining room, or through a television set.

"If you haven't read that book, you have to read it first. It was the first book he wrote and it didn't just make him famous—it made him a phenomenon. Up until it led to his suicide. It was too much for him—he couldn't go out in the street or to any restaurant, any hotel in the world. When he came to eat here, I told him, 'Thank you so much.' He got here, parked the car, filmed the segment and told me, 'My crew tells me this is the best food they've ever had in the entire time I've been with them, and those motherfuckers eat!' The two times they came, I fed them."

"In the background though, he wasn't happy," Julio said.

Right, Lalo said. From the surface, it seemed like he had everything—love, money, admiration. "But he couldn't say, 'that's enough.' He couldn't say, 'that's enough.'"

No one could know just what happened to Bourdain, Lalo said. But he had planned for a future that he didn't live.

The job could kill you, one way or another. Maybe a blood vessel would burst in your brain. Maybe your desire would fade as your body began to deteriorate. Maybe the market would grow frigid, and you would watch your customers' tastes change, as they grew bored with what they had once celebrated.

Before his death, Bourdain gave a speech for students graduating from the Culinary School of America and urged chefs to change. *Kitchen Confidential* portrayed the drug-addled, adrenaline-fueled culture of restaurant kitchens in the 1990s; his electric prose and dark humor gave the lifestyle sex appeal, but seventeen years later, he was repentant. "What kind of place do we want to work in? What kind of behavior will we accept in our presence?" Bourdain asked the graduates. "This is why so many people in our industry are fucked up."

When Lalo looked across the table at Julio, he saw determination, but also a fragility that scared him.

"Plant and grow radishes, if that's what gives you satisfaction!" Lalo said.

But Julio was unshakeable. He was working out four or five hours a day. "People look at me like I'm crazy. But it's for *me*. It's because I want to be well. I'm *going* to be."

"Listen, everything you do from now on—and this is going to sound really selfish, but it's not—do it for yourself," Lalo said. "Don't do it for your wife. Don't do it for your mother. Don't do it for absolutely anyone else. At the end of the day, if you don't help yourself, then other people are only going to support you up to a point, and then they won't be there. Your wife has to live her life, she has to work. So, whatever you do, do it for you. And then, when you're at 100 percent and you want to help someone else, help them! You understand?"

Julio promised to come back for another visit. Lalo returned to the kitchen. It was close to lunch service on a Wednesday and the reservation book was half-empty. Lalo was worried. It seemed like the restaurant wasn't as full as it used to be. But Gaby was the numbers person and, according to her, things were doing just fine. "I don't see it," Lalo said.

Some members of the team were solid, of course, but it seemed like every six months, several of the cooks had to be replaced. Sometimes, they were fired. More often, they left because they grew tired of the difficult boss and the pace of the work, or because they found other opportunities.

In earlier years, service would find Lalo singing snatches of songs that were piped through the dining room speakers. "Fly Me to the Moon," "Ya Me Voy Para Siempre," "Get Ur Freak On," "Band on the Run."

Did he still sing the way he used to?

"No," he said. "Because the right people are not around me."

At times, Lalo felt a tingling in his head. His nerves were being tested and he'd inch close to an explosion. He'd try to take things down a notch. He'd breathe and tell one of the waiters to fetch him a gin and tonic. When it arrived, a thin slice of grapefruit floating jauntily over the ice, he could glimpse for a split second what it was to be one of the customers, indulging in a mid-afternoon cocktail. He'd take a sip and remind himself of the people depending on him.

He traveled as often as he could justify the time away. But unlike his colleagues, he couldn't jump on a plane to Austin to see what was new on the barbecue scene. Gaby's sister had moved to France's Loire Valley, and they'd often journey around the continent with a stop to see her.

"They're serving this everywhere in France right now," Lalo said as he plated a beef and vegetable soup at Havre 77, his classical French spot.

"And in Chicanburris," one of the waiters replied. Chicanburris was the slang waiters had brought to Lalo's restaurant from Pujol, for a town in the middle of nowhere. Podunk, Mexico.

The new Máximo would require more hires, and as he welcomed people onto his team, Lalo told them about the larger kitchen and the top-of-the-line appliances, elements he hoped would boost morale. He and Gaby had also taken another bold step in recent years: they had given a few of their employees part-ownership. They had done this in exchange for nothing, hoping the investment would ulti- mately yield a return by creating a change in a common restaurant dynamic that had plagued them since the beginning: the turnover rate. The most talented members of the team eventually left to learn more, travel more, or open their own restaurants. If those who had proven their commitment were rewarded with ownership, the way they understood their part in the business might change. They would own the restaurant's failure as well as its success. That sense of responsibility would trickle down in the way they managed the rest of the staff. They would push the team forward even when Lalo and Gaby were physically absent. And maybe, someday, the couple could step aside, before Lalo's body broke.

That year, Lalo and Gaby decided to self-publish a cookbook with Vivian Bibliowicz, a Colombian photographer and food writer living in Mexico. It was a way to commemorate the old Máximo Bistrot before it shuttered, and featured photographs of the staff of the restaurant as well as the food. Working with Bibliowicz, Lalo wrote a short essay about his cooking. "Even though I don't see myself as an innovator, I cook and I build my own language. I taste things in my mind and I choose the ingredients that start a conversation with the kind of food I like," he wrote. "Technique you can learn. But flavor you've got to live."

The book included short profiles of the Mexican purveyors who supplied the restaurant's ingredients, with stunning photographs of the kitchen's raw materials and the final results. But it was remarkable for another reason. Though Lalo didn't often talk about Max in his day-to-day, Lalo dedicated the book to him. In its introductory pages he explained the connection between his son and the restaurant, saying that his life's work had been and would continue to be for Max. "It's important to me that he knows I never forgot him, will never forget him and—even if he chooses to have nothing to do with me or ever count on my support—I will be there." If he wanted to get in touch, Lalo would be waiting "with open arms."

Lalo had loved the physicality of cooking, of filleting a fresh fish and turning it into a crisp and buttery thing of beauty in the sauté pan. He loved whisking eggs with a steady stream of oil until they emulsified into mayonnaise. He loved barreling through the kitchen crying "*Caliente!*" as he moved a fifty-pound pot of veal stock. Those quotidian actions once strengthened him. Now, the momentum reversed course: his bones splintered, his memory faded, his liver yellowed. In the din of the kitchen, he hushed his body's plaintive aches and summoned his food, which spoke with its own lucid voice.

NOTES ON A PLAGUE

In February, Charles de Lisle told them to get ready. This virus, this *bichito*, wasn't about a lean month or a difficult first quarter. It could be the end of their businesses. The profit margins were already slim—around 3 to 5 percent; no matter how much money you had, the overhead of operating an empty restaurant would gobble it down and then wait for the next course: debt.

On the originally designated opening day for the new Máximo— March 22, 2020—schools in Mexico had been suspended and large gatherings banned. There were 316 confirmed cases of the novel coronavirus in the country. Nearly 15,000 deaths had been documented around the world. Lalo and Gaby sat at a table in the empty dining room wearing N95 masks they'd procured through a contact as they mulled over scenarios. Gaby preached patience and caution. There was a lot they still didn't know, and that meant it was too soon to act decisively.

When they finally opened their doors in early July, the mandate *quedate en casa*, or stay at home, had cleared commuter traffic from the streets and the city air felt cleansed, like it had quit a smoking habit. By then, 28,000 deaths had been confirmed in Mexico. Lalo was cooking, correcting, walking circles through the vast kitchen. The pantry shelves were stocked with glass canisters of leathery guajillo chiles, star anise, and burnt vanilla. Bunches of chamomile and branches of eucalyptus hung from the posts of the walls in the dining room. De Lisle's vision of casual elegance had prevailed; the new restaurant nodded to local culture and the natural world. A few of the features recalled the tree of life that had been prominently displayed in the original Máximo: plaster sculptures of a bird and Easter lilies were embossed on the walls, and a live tree stood in the center of the dining room, reaching toward the sun. The facade of the building was understated—a gray wall of concrete, with rough volcanic rock jutting through. It recalled the farmhouses in the village where Lalo was born, cement-fortified stone structures molded by time and use. In the entryway, six gold letters told customers they were in the right place: Máximo.

This was, of course, not the opening Gaby and Lalo had hoped for when they stood in that muddy former pool hall and imagined what they might create. The new restaurant was supposed to be a backdrop for relaxed dinners that would stretch into the dawn hours, a place where people forgot about the time and the price of the wine and ordered another glass. The waiters looked sharp in their new khaki uniforms, but as they huddled for a final briefing, they spoke through black masks and looked at one another through safety goggles. At the door, a thermometer gun checked temperatures upon arrival. The kitchen was visible through a massive window as guests walked through the entrance toward the dining room, putting the cooks on heightened display. They pushed soapy water across the floor and polished the countertops one more time.

In Mexico City, the colors red, orange, yellow, and green came to signify the severity of restrictions in place, based on hospital bed occupancy. On opening day, the city was on *semaforo naranja*— code orange. Restaurants were allowed to open at reduced capacity, and Máximo's new protocols reflected city regulations. Research emerged confirming that the virus was airborne and indicating that transmission was more likely indoors; walking into this refined space was infused with trepidation.

They waited for cues from on high about loans or forgiveness on late rent. In his daily press conferences, President López Obrador was insouciant. For months, he appeared at events maskless, traveling and greeting admirers with gusto. "You have to hug, nothing happens," he said. "Don't lie, steal or betray, that helps a lot to avoid getting the coronavirus." He showed off his good luck charms: a four-leafed clover and a two-dollar bill. The government issued a daily barrage of updates but officially downplayed the importance of testing, rendering the authority of their information suspect.

Restaurants across the city fell behind on rent. More than 13,000 shuttered. Those that held on watched their savings slip away. The founders of Masala y Maíz, a trailblazing restaurant that brought together Mexican and Indian concepts, continued to pay their employees and went into debt. Chef Norma Listman-Sánchez panicked as the government froze her bank account, a penalty for owing thousands of dollars in taxes. "In Mexico you get punished for doing the right thing," she told a reporter. "The people who fired all of their employees at the beginning don't owe all of the taxes that I owe."

In the early days of the pandemic, Máximo couldn't seat diners at all—they could only sell food to go. Customers with the means took home lavish meals of lamb, artichokes, and tarte tatin. At Lalo!, their casual spot, they sold a gourmet grocery list. All in all, they were bringing in 5 to 8 percent of their former earnings. For the skeleton crew who reported to the restaurant, work was tinged with fear of exposure to the virus, but it was also a distraction, a way to prevent themselves from leaning into anxiety. Chef de partie Andrés Trujillo and head pastry chef Vanessa Franco, Venezuelans who became a couple during their years cooking at Máximo, were the first to come to Lalo and ask to continue working. Together, they learned to make food that would survive in transit and present well on the home table. They arrived at the restaurant at dawn and went home after dark; their coloring faded to a vampiric pallor. Along with Lalo and two other cooks, they took turns doing the grunt work of washing dishes and preparing mis en place. No one knew just what they were risking by feeding a few rich people and trying to keep the businesses from going under.

The Central de Abasto, the square-mile market where the city's restaurants and smaller markets buy supplies daily, became a coronavirus hotspot. More than a year later, no census had been taken of how many workers in the market had died, or the number of cases. "There was no oversight, but there were thousands of cases, that's for certain," said Agustin Rodríguez, the secretary of the market's workers alliance. Merchants were reluctant to report ill employees—if they did, they were forced to close their stands. But it was obvious to Rodríguez and his fellow vendors that the market "was a huge center of contagion. It was ugly, very ugly." When the pandemic ended, Lalo expected, the workers now being called "essential" would be forgotten.

As tens of thousands of businesses closed, as desperate pleas for oxygen tanks went out to family members, then were forwarded to friends and strangers, as 130,000 Mexican children woke up to a childhood defined by the loss of a parent, López Obrador stuck to his dictum of austerity. Around 40 percent of Mexicans lived in poverty before the pandemic, and he refused to plunge his country into debt in the name of Covid relief, or abandon the programs he'd campaigned on. There were a few concessions—money for funerals, microloans to small businesses. In the Cuauhtémoc borough, where Máximo was located, restaurants received enough from the local government to pay their employees for two weeks' labor. The federal government's main priority was to secure vaccines from Russia, the United States, China, and the United Kingdom to immunize the population. Like most Mexicans, Gaby continued to support the president through the crisis. The rich might hate him, but Mexico wasn't a rich country. It was time to be less greedy, she felt, and put the interests of others above their own.

Around the city, restaurant workers lost their jobs with meager public assistance to support them through unemployment—2,742 pesos, or around $130 per month for four months. The paperwork was so onerous that most people didn't bother to enroll. There were one-off assistance programs scattered around the country—Mexico was approaching an election year and politicians were in competition for their votes—but the help was piecemeal. Theoretically, Mexican law guaranteed workers severance upon losing a long-term job, but enforcing the law was another story. Conditions were ripe for worker abuse, with a broken unemployment system, low salaries, and limited access to justice. A lawsuit could easily languish for five years before a worker saw her day in court.

Lalo and Gaby continued to pay their employees, albeit a reduced salary. Many of the waiters went to Acatepec, their hometown in southern Puebla, and spent a few months with their families in the houses they'd built over the years. One opened a butcher shop and, happy he could spend all week with his family after years of seeing them once every ten days, quit waiting tables.

Máximo had better odds than most restaurants. It was a highly successful business, and Lalo and Gaby had savings, along with lawyers and investment managers to help them make smart decisions. Still, the timing could not have been worse: along with their partners, they had poured more than two million dollars into the new restaurant. In 2019, Gaby had rolled her eyes and smiled as Lalo insisted on spending another $50,000 on top-of-the-line hoods for the kitchen, as de Lisle insisted on another $100,000 for custommade overhead lights from an Italian designer. Now, their ultimate survival seemed to depend on the return of the very hospitality they had extended through their businesses. Would the landlord be kind enough to accept delayed rent? Would the employees suffer through pay cuts? Would the customers buy gift cards for a future meal that might not come? Not all of these were simple acts of kindness; they involved their own calculations. If landlords threw out their tenants, who would rent the storefronts in a depressed economy? If the staff refused to take a pay cut, would there be a restaurant for them to work at once the restrictions were lifted?

Lalo broke his time into segments to get through the day, like he had in prison. Gaby found solace in yoga and meditation. They were both drinking every night. Before the pandemic, Lalo had daydreamed about a world upended, one that might offer him the excuse to escape to a simpler life. But when the upside-down future arrived, it hit differently. The exits were suddenly blocked: no flight to a European vacation spot, no guarantee of health or safety anywhere on Earth. All he needed was Gaby, and the assurance that his family was safe. But even if they could leave, they had a hundred people depending on them to make it to the other side. A hundred people, each with their own family, petrified of what tomorrow would look like and who they would say goodbye to through a tinny cell phone speaker, or if they would be the intubated patient on the other end of the call.

When he saw conspiracy theories posted on social media, Lalo couldn't help but think there was a purpose to the chaos. The world was suffering under the burden of too many people addicted to fossil fuels. Success depended on martyrdom; a recalibration of values was in order.

Natalia came to visit right before the pandemic began, and then got stuck. She isolated in the house in the Estado de México, where she planted an ambitious vegetable garden and spent the endless days cleaning and tending to her plants. Back in the U.S., Maria, Isela, and their families came down with Covid. Maria's case was the most severe, and she struggled to recover her former vitality. Then, she was injured in a car accident, which prevented her from returning to her waitressing job for almost a year. Lalo's earnings were more needed than ever.

ICUs remained full, but political will shifted: restrictions eased and the *semaforo* blinked from red to orange to yellow. Máximo saw its audience come back. What did the colors mean anymore? What did Covid do to the body? When would the pandemic end? No one knew the answers. Mexico became an escape for foreigners tired of more restrictive policies in their home countries. Despite the city's official recommendation to wear masks, these tourists walked the streets unencumbered, filling outdoor seating that mushroomed into the parking lane. Máximo went from busy to fully booked.

Lalo got tested for Covid throughout 2020. Something wasn't right. He was languid and his stomach was off. The tests came back negative, and doctors kept diagnosing him with various probable causes. Finally, one afternoon in December, it was Gaby who felt unwell. A hangover, she figured. So, she drank some more, her new custom for blocking out the stress. By nightfall every inch of her body ached, and the sheets were drenched with sweat. Lalo wrapped her in a hug. "*No tienes Covid,*" he assured her for the hundredth time in a year of scares and near misses; she had a positive test in hand by the time he and Natalia began to feel symptoms two days later. They shut down the restaurant, which had a small cluster of cases, and quarantined at home. One of the longtime waiters, Rubén Luna Rivera, fell desperately ill. His first and principal symptom was pain; it began in his knees, then radiated up his legs and through his back. Even so, he convinced himself it was a cold and finished his shift. Then, he lost his sense of smell, a surefire sign of Covid. At a public health clinic they gave him paracetamol, another pack of pills, and an injection, "of what, I don't know." He looked around at his empty apartment. How would he feed himself? How would he survive? He decided to chance the drive to be with his wife, five hours away in Acatepec. He stopped at toll booths and gas stations to stretch and sleep as he struggled to breathe and fight a fever, too tired to be afraid. His wife prepared a room for him to isolate in, and made him teas infused with eucalyptus and rosemary to soothe his throat and open his lungs; as he grew stronger, she prepared fresh juices and *atole de avena.* He recovered and returned to work three weeks later.

Gaby and Natalia recovered quickly. Lalo's case seemed light, and he was especially grateful to have never lost his sense of smell or taste, but, as time went on, he continued to feel sluggish. At first, doctors said he must have long Covid, but he'd felt this way months before his positive result. Blood draws, scans, a biopsy, and then a diagnosis: nonalcoholic steatohepatitis—fatty liver disease. Or, as he put it, "foie gras." He cut out alcohol, meat, sweets, and began an exercise regimen. He dropped forty pounds in a couple of months, shaved the final remnants of hair from his head, and came to resemble a chef–athlete. He still spent his days surrounded by butter, pâté, and champagne, but it was all forbidden. He didn't seem to mind: "I'd rather live." None of the doctors who treated him mentioned that emerging research suggests a link between exposure to the insecticide glyphosate, the principal ingredient in Monsanto's weed killer Roundup—which was in widespread use when Lalo and his family worked the fields—and fatty liver disease.

By the summer of 2021, the crisis seemed to be closer to the end than the beginning. Now that they and their families and employees were vaccinated, now that the new Máximo was so in-demand they decided to open every day of the week, that urge to "run, run, run" returned to Lalo with a vengeance. They couldn't leave, of course. There were investors to repay, workers to support, a vision to see through to fruition. As in the U.S., it was growing difficult to find kitchen staff, but not all of the reasons were the same: the cooks who had stayed with them through the pandemic were leaving for a rush of new opportunities to staff restaurants in Mexico, the U.S., Europe. Or they were starting something of their own. Máximo, along with Alinea, Le Bernardin, and Eleven Madison Park, posted on Instagram in search of talent.

All the while, Lalo was at the height of his powers. Before his diagnosis, the pandemic had prompted him to cook comfort food. After they reopened, he put fried chicken coated with barbecue sauce on the menu, and a *sincronizada de birria de lechón*—stewed and shredded pork folded into a tortilla, encased in cheese, and grilled on the comal. Then there were the new dishes that went to the opposite extreme—unfamiliar, inventive indulgences. A landrace corn and porcini mushroom soup with a soft-shell crab crisp on the side for dipping. Plantain bread with macadamia nuts, served warm and fragrant from the oven, topped with crème fraiche, red onion, and an abundance of caviar. The dish was inspired by a small plate created by René Redzepi for one of Pujol's anniversaries—a thin slice of raw banana brushed with vanilla bean and vanilla oil, covered with a confetti of shaved macadamia nuts, then piled with caviar. The bite contained everything Lalo loved: a harmonious, balanced blend of flavors, round on the palate, including banana, his favorite fruit, the fresh, briny pop of caviar, the faint perfume of vanilla, and finally buttery macadamia, one of the Mexican-sourced ingredients he'd thrilled in adding to his repertoire when he opened Máximo. Lalo's version looked nothing like Redzepi's—it was essentially a homey baked good coupled with a heady dip in the ocean. Totally unexpected, and totally delicious.

Andrés Trujillo and Vanessa Franco left Máximo in May of 2021, after being offered a chance to open a new restaurant at a boutique resort in Baja California, where they could design the menu with creative freedom. Trujillo had worked at Máximo for nearly six years. When he began, he was the line cook tripping over his feet as he tried to follow Lalo's instructions in the heat of the dinner rush. Over time, he had graduated to competence, and, finally, mastery through thousands of hours of dedicated work. Franco, who was a genius with desserts before she ever walked through the doors of Máximo, was likewise a single-minded perfectionist, dedicated to her craft with ravenous intensity. Lalo could execute a good tart or ice cream, to be sure, but he stood in awe of Franco. With her arrival, the restaurant's desserts manifested the beauty, originality, and exceptional technique seen on the main menu. "She understands the simplicity of flavors," Lalo said. It was a seemingly understated compliment, but to Lalo that aptitude was indicative of a mind–palate connection, the distinguishing factor between a cook and a chef. He told anyone who was interested that Franco was the most talented chef to have ever worked for him.

When the pair learned of the opportunity to move on, they told Lalo first. They'd watched employees of the past depart on uneasy terms; even if Lalo didn't approve of the offer or wished they would stay, if they were honest with him, they knew he would be supportive. Even so, when Lalo stood up in front of the dining room on their last day and pronounced them two of the most important people to have ever worked for the restaurant, they were stunned. Trujillo had never seen him make such a gesture. He attributed it to a maturation—in himself, as a young cook taking the job seriously, and in Lalo. Far from Venezuela, Máximo had given them a new place to call home. "We took care of it the best we could."

Trujillo and Franco shared Lalo's drive to be the best, not as ordained by an award committee, but by one's own standards. Where others saw a dusty relic, Trujillo saw merit in the hierarchical system of culinary training. For a technique to become second nature, to obtain the sensitivity to perform in a gesture what an early-career chef might labor over, you had to repeat basic skills ad nauseam, in a defined order.

"Let's say you learn to play piano today, and you learn a song. So you practice it, repeat it and repeat it, and you get to the point where you say, 'Wow, I played this song so nicely.' Imagine if I taught you that song when you've played piano for twenty years. How fast do you think you'd learn it? In a second? That's how you understand a craftsman like him."

In the spring of 2021, as restaurants in the U.S. struggled to draw workers back to physically and psychologically draining jobs, restaurant workers in Mexico began to protest their treatment on social media. Hundreds of restaurants across the country were denounced for paying less than minimum wage, sexual harassment, putting employees in danger by skirting protocols, and forcing workers to sign blank sheets of paper, which could be used to forge letters of resignation—a worker who resigned was not entitled to the same severance pay as someone who was fired. Máximo Bistrot received anonymous accusations from two employees and Pujol became a focus of allegations, with Enrique Olvera pledging to examine conditions for his employees.

Some young cooks recognized an opportunity afoot to create something new, to reject the old systems and speak with their own voices directly to the consumer. They hadn't put in a decade of painstaking work like Trujillo, but they had other skills. They were fluent in the language of virality, they knew how to conjure camera-ready recipes and shoot professional-quality images with their phones that would be salivated over and shared with a string of exclamation points and emojis. They might not have attended culinary school, but they'd read and tasted widely. Their food was explicitly connected to their politics, their heritage, their environmental activism. They got their products to consumers by any means necessary. A chef delivered his cooking kits of hand-ground curries by bicycle. A couple began a baking business with a $42 toaster oven. A menu-less collective prepared experimental tacos, sopes, and tlacoyos made from landrace corn. Customers lined up without a single paid advertisement. These young cooks were adapting to the conditions of the pandemic, too—food could be taken to go, seating was primarily outdoors, menus were accessed via QR code. No need to invest in elaborate dining rooms or train servers. They were working fewer days, shorter hours, keeping overhead low. They were setting the terms for what a sustainable career might look like. They were a small cohort, but they were making their voices heard.

You could call it a trend, but was it new? Tens of thousands of inventive vendors with street carts, stands, and fondas fed the city delicacies from across the republic every day, peripatetic purveyors announcing "*tamales zacahuiiiiil*" wrapped in banana leaves, or barrels of *tepache*, a lightly effervescent drink made of fermented pineapple skin, piloncillo, and cinnamon. On street corners, snack food artists split open bags of Doritos and layered them with pickled pork rinds, peanuts, chamoy, and jicama. And then there were the simplest pleasures, the old standbys: a sweaty *taco de canasta*; a mango sculpted into the shape of a blooming rose; a sweet potato roasted in a charcoal oven for a warm treat on a rainy night. Lalo's favorite stand sold quesadillas with chorizo. They reminded him of the ones his grandfather had made during his childhood summers in San José de las Pilas.

Lalo wasn't sure how long he'd stay in the city. He had the new, expansive kitchen with top-of-the-line appliances. He could accommodate a more robust staff to complete the day's tasks in a more orderly fashion. But something still needed to change. To manage the kitchen professionally, he admitted, "I need help." He posted a video on Instagram: an animated man in a suit and tie runs toward a bundle of dollar bills suspended in front of him. As he runs, his body disintegrates, the money flies out of view, and his skeleton collapses into a grave.

Money was no longer a problem. The restaurant was packed—every day felt like Saturday. They were flooded with new customers: a backlog of tourists eager to celebrate the end of isolation and spend their dollars, and a new population of remote workers who had moved to the city now that they were no longer obliged to report to an office. Plus, their local customers, who had spent the past year at home, were venturing out again and wanted to see the new location. Against all odds, Lalo and Gaby had come out of the pandemic more successful than they had dreamed possible. With that anxiety allayed, Lalo had found a new challenge he was impatient to confront: after a decade of cultivating his creativity through practice, travel, and experimentation, he sensed that he'd approached the outer limits of what he could achieve through self-directed study. When he was young, Michele Sedgwick, then Enrique Olvera, had challenged him to move beyond his predilections. Now, he longed to fill the gaps in his education. To study, with humility, what an Italian grandmother might teach him about pasta. To be the child in the classroom who pays attention to the words on the chalkboard because he knows the language the teacher is speaking. To shape those nouns and adjectives into a sonnet.

It had been fourteen years since Lalo was last deported from the United States. He wasn't allowed to return, even for a visit. He was jealous of colleagues who could take a weekend trip to visit farm-to-kitchen restaurants in New England, or to see how Creole chefs in New Orleans were rethinking sustainable seafood, and he looked askance at those who had the chance to make these journeys but didn't—what a waste! But mostly, his disappointments centered on his separation from Max, and his dreams of a possible reunion.

In September of 2021, Lalo and Gaby bought a piece of land in the countryside, surrounded by old-growth pine trees with a view of a lake. It was near a wealthy resort area, but just far enough from it to raise the question of whether potential customers would be willing to make the trip. They wanted to open an inn, a place where people could learn about the value of ethically grown food, take cooking classes, eat good meals, and rest. His cooks could train there before beginning work at Máximo, the management of which he and Gaby hoped to leave in other hands. They would learn to grow corn, to plow a field, to forage for mushrooms. For now, it was just an idea, one of many, but it proved to be the most persistent. If the right moment came, this new venture wouldn't represent a break from the past, nor would it be a homecoming. Lalo wouldn't resolve the contradictions of the food system in which he'd labored. He wouldn't abandon it, either. There, in the forest, Lalo might find a place where the knowledge of his experiences could be given new form.

ACKNOWLEDGMENTS

I had many collaborators on this journey, without whom this project would not have been possible.

Thank you to the staff of Máximo Bistrot, who graciously answered my questions over months and years, and made space for me in the kitchen. Special thanks to Oscar Luna Rivera, Gisela Arotoma, Andrés Trujillo, Federico Ríos, Juan Escalona Meléndez, Gabriel Rodríguez, and Mariana Alfarache. Thank you also to the staff of Peyote Dubai, especially Roberto Rivera, Francisco Omaña, and Crystal Sánchez.

I had the pleasure of interviewing many great chefs to better understand a changing city and how it was reflected in a changing cuisine. Thank you to Mónica Patiño, Enrique Olvera, Jorge Vallejo, Alejandro Ruiz, Gabriela Cámara, Norma Listman-Sánchez, and Martha Ortiz for sharing their experiences with me. I'll always be grateful for the opportunities I had to interview the late Yuri de Gortari Krauss and Diana Kennedy. Thank you to Elena Reygadas, who allowed me to spend three weeks working alongside the talented chefs in the pastry kitchen of her restaurant Rosetta.

Thank you to the many writers and thinkers who shared their deep knowledge of subjects that are only briefly touched upon in these pages: Gustavo Arellano, Sarah Bak-Geller Corona, Alyshia Gálvez, David Tavárez, Cynthia Rice, Paulina Oliva, Ruth Reichl, Tina Shull, John Kessler, Carly Goodman, Heidi Castaneda, Alonso Ruvalcaba, Deborah Harris, Jorge Durand, José Antonio Vásquez-Medina, Andrew Haley, Roberto Cruz Peña, Francisco Musi, Christopher Hart, Alejandro Hope, Hamanth Gundavaram, Paul Freedman, Lauren Joyner, Cynthia Greenlee, Jeannie Economos, Stephen Bright, Rachel Miller, Douglas Massey, Enrique Sepúlveda, Lucio Usobiaga, and Mark Overmyer-Velázquez for your time, reading recommendations, and insight. Thank you to Latino USA and the Institute for Journalism and Natural Resources for supporting related research on pesticide exposure among the children of migrant farmworkers. Thank you to the Catwalk Art Residency for a productive and restorative stay.

Thank you to my agent, Jacqueline Ko, who supported this project long before there was anything to show on the page, and my editor, Melanie Tortoroli, who offered just the right balance of clarity and freedom to get it to the end. Thank you both for your patience and belief in the importance of Lalo's story. Thank you to Mo Crist, for pushing the project ahead at a critical moment. Thank you to the staff of W. W. Norton, including Annabel Brazaitis, Susan Sanfrey, and Will Scarlett, and to proofreader Vivian Reinert. Thank you also to Richard Ljeones for the cover design, and to photographer Mallika Vora. Thank you to Angely Mercado and copyeditor Allegra Huston, for your diligent work. To Andrew Wylie, thank you for being in my corner.

To Theo Emery, José Luis Chicoma, Tom French, Oscar Cásares, Larry Cohen, Cyntia González Santos, Whitney Eulich, Michael D'Antonio, Robin Myers, Daniel Loedel, Susette Brooks, Suzannah Lessard, Hannah de Keijzer, David Tillman, Adam Williams, Allegra Ben-Amotz, Lydia Carey, and Ellie Bozmarova, thank you for reading. Some of you looked at a single chapter, others the whole manuscript. Thank you each for your invaluable feedback during different stages of this project. Special thanks to Suzannah Lessard for your iconoclastic guidance and your friendship. Thank you to Tracy Kidder for a significant early chat about immersive reporting. To the late Dick Todd, your love of writing made me want to do this again. Thank you always.

To Lalo's family—particularly to Natalia, Maria, and Gaby—thank you for sharing your stories with me.

To Lalo, without whom there is no book. Thank you for answering my endless questions; thank you for your commitment to seeing this through; thank you for sharing your life. Learning from you has indelibly shaped the way I look at my own.

To our *vecinidad* in the Roma Sur, for being by my side through joy and grief. To the inhabitants of E2. To Yvette and Lindsay—I'm so glad we went out to dinner that night. To my parents, Maureen and Wayne, and my brother David for your encouragement and love. To Lulu, whose hard work helping to care for our children made it all possible. To Chris, for helping me get through the thorniest patches, for celebrating the good things. And to Augie and Willa, the food critics at our family table, who came into the world while this book was being reported. I'm so lucky to be your mama.

NOTES

A note regarding reporting challenges: Lalo's memory of his early years is complicated by the itinerant nature of his time as a migrant farmworker; Natalia's memory has been impacted by trauma. While Maria has a good memory of the family's life in Chamblee and in the Estado de México, she was not present during the majority of their time as migrant farmworkers. Lupe is no longer alive. This has presented obstacles to verifying certain pieces of information. Many of these instances are noted individually below. Some prison and immigration records were available as a cross-reference, and whenever possible I sought out multiple sources to corroborate individual memories with other family members or friends. I also spoke with experts and read scholarship on these subjects in order to put Lalo's recollections into context. In a few cases, figures from Lalo's life declined to be interviewed or could not be located.

Prologue

xvi **named one of the fifty best in Latin America, the best in Mexico:** The World's 50 Best Restaurants, which curates a set of lists that rank restaurants around the world, has included Máximo Bistrot on their Latin America list on several occasions. In 2022, Máximo was named 89th best restaurant in the world, according to their extended list. Máximo won the top category at the 2018 Gourmet Awards in Mexico, and was awarded the highest rating in Mexico City in the 2013 Zagat guide.

xvii **a lanky ten-year-old:** There is some uncertainty among Lalo and his family about the exact age at which he began working in the U.S. Based on family memories, it's estimated he was nine or ten years old.

Chapter One: Tortillas at Dawn

1 **doesn't appear on a state map:** San José de las Pilas is located in the municipality of Acámbaro, Guanajuato, close to the border of the state of Michoacán. Searching for Acámbaro will provide a rough location of where Lalo was born. His village is not to be confused with a larger town in Guanajuato also called San José de las Pilas, located about 100 kilometers to the north, which pops up when one searches for the name.

4 **bring the boys, now ten and eight:** The family isn't completely certain which year this took place, but their best guess is 1988, based on the memories of an uncle who helped pay a coyote for their safe passage. By then, Natalia says, Lupe had his green card and could travel freely between the countries.

5 **part of the Bracero Program:** For more on the program, visit bracero archive.org and pick up historian Mireya Loza's book *Defiant Braceros: How Migrant Workers Fought for Racial, Sexual and Political Freedom* (Chapel Hill: University of North Carolina Press, 2016), which further complicates the narrative. Loza's research informs this section.

6 **Henry Pope Anderson put it this way:** Lori A. Flores, "A Town Full of Dead Mexicans: The Salinas Valley Tragedy of 1963, The End of the Bracero Program, and the Evolution of the Chicano Movement," *Western Historical Quarterly* 44, no. 2 (2013): 124–43.

6 **Great Strike Wave of 1946:** As Melvyn Dubofsky writes, in 1946 "almost 5,000 strikes affected 4.6 million workers," which constituted more than 10 percent of all U.S. workers at the time. Melvyn Dubofsky, "Labor Unrest in the United States, 1906–90," *Review (Fernand Braudel Center)* 18, no. 1 (1995): 125–35, http://www.jstor.org/stable/40241326.

6 **Congress dominated by white Southern Democrats had crafted the exclusion:** Legal historian Juan F. Perea writes, "Specifically, southern congressmen wanted to exclude black employees from the New Deal to preserve the quasi-plantation style of agriculture that pervaded the still-segregated Jim Crow South. While they supported reforms that would bring more prosperity to their relatively poor region, they rejected those that might upset the existing system of racial segregation and exploitation of blacks." He concludes that the continued existence of the exclusion is,

first, "a remarkably effective way to create and preserve racial caste. Second, race-neutral language has been and can be used purposefully to inflict racially targeted harm upon politically vulnerable groups. It is only our temporal distance from the crafting of this exclusion that even permits us to deem it 'race-neutral.' Its authors, as well as those most affected by the exclusion, knew it to be anything but neutral." Today, these exclusions, "originally intended to keep blacks impoverished and subservient now keep Latino farm and domestic workers subservient." Juan F. Perea, "The Echoes of Slavery: Recognizing the Racist Origins of the Agricultural and Domestic Worker Exclusion from the National Labor Relations Act," *Ohio State Law Journal* 72, no. 1 (2011): 95–138.

7   **taxing, grimy, poisonous:** Two decades before Lalo came to the U.S., Truman E. Moore provided this exercise for urban Americans trying to imagine life in a migrant camp, in his chronicle of migrant workers and their conditions, *The Slaves We Rent* (New York: Random House, 1965): "In the middle of your living room, mark off a space eight feet wide and sixteen feet long. This represents half of a two-family cabin in a Princeton, Florida, camp where a thousand migrants live during the season. Here two families live in a cabin sixteen feet square. If you put a few chairs in the space you have marked off, you begin to see how a room can close in. Try spending an evening in it. But imagine while you sit there that on the other side of a one-inch wall sits another family. When they walk around, your side of the cabin shakes."

7   **their skin made sticky with the chemicals:** According to Cynthia Rice, a California Rural Legal Assistance attorney who represents migrant farmworkers, pesticide exposure—including direct contact with insecticides—remains a threat to workers, and their overall treatment is contemptible. As Rice put it, "We pay far more attention to what's put on the food in the fields than to what the workers are subjected to who work with that food."

9   **Natalia, born Salome García Acevedo:** Natalia wasn't aware that her given name was Salome until adulthood; she's gone by Natalia her entire life.

11   **Nixtamalization changes the chemical properties of corn:** A diet primarily based on corn can result in the wasting disease pellagra. According to the *Encyclopedia of Human Nutrition*, "the niacin present in corn and other grains is often chemically bound into a macromolecular complex that is sometimes called niacytin, from which the niacin cannot readily be released by digestive enzymes in the gastrointestinal tract but which requires heat and alkali treatment during food preparation (as in the preparation of Mexican tortillas, which involves lime and heat treatment) so as to make it adequately bioavailable." In places where corn has been the basis of the local diet but is not processed with calcium, pellagra results in a scaly rash, diarrhea, and dementia, along with other neurological symptoms. As corn was introduced

to other regions of the globe, absent of the accompanying technique of nix-tamalization, pellagra became a common consequence. See https://www.sciencedirect.com/topics/medicine-and-dentistry/pellagra.

13 **most everything that Lalo and Jaime did was illegal:** An interview with Michael Hancock, the former director of Farmworker Justice and former assistant administrator for the Department of Labor's Wage and Hour Division, helped establish where Lalo and Jaime's work fell in terms of labor regulation. Hancock also detailed the norms of child labor, including the inevitability of children working in agricultural fields when their parents have no access to childcare.

15 **a bunch of kids approached them:** Jaime remembered being called "onion boy" by other children. Lalo says that, as an adult, these interactions stuck with him. "I don't know why, but I still think about it, sometimes a couple times a week."

16 **Then came the eugenics movement:** For further reading on eugenics, see Lulu Miller's "Why Fish Don't Exist," which focuses on Stanford president David Starr Jordan, a prominent eugenicist.

16 **Instead, farmers changed crops:** Michael A. Clemens, Ethan G. Lewis, and Hannah M. Postel, "Immigration Restrictions as Active Labor Market Policy: Evidence from the Mexican Bracero Exclusion," *American Economic Review* 108, no. 6 (2017): 1468–87.

17 **recruiting high school athletes:** For the complete story, see Gustavo Arellano, "When the U.S. Government Tried to Replace Braceros with High Schoolers," NPR, August 23, 2018, https://www.npr.org/sections/thesalt/2018/07/31/634442195/when-the-u-s-government-tried-to-replace-migrant-farmworkers-with-high-schoolers.

17 **farmworkers came together to protest:** United Farm Workers, "The Rise of the UFW," https://ufw.org/research/history/ufw-history, accessed June 1, 2020; Adam Janos, "How Cesar Chavez Joined Larry Itliong to Demand Farm Workers' Rights," History.com, https://www.history.com/news/chavez-itliong-delano-grape-strike.

17 **Cesar Chavez, was initially unwelcoming to foreign-born migrants:** See Miriam Pawel, *The Crusades of Cesar Chavez* (New York: Bloomsbury, 2014), and Lori A. Flores, *Grounds for Dreaming: Mexican Americans, Mexican Immigrants, and the California Farmworker Movement* (New Haven: Yale University Press, 2016).

17 **less than 1 percent of farmworkers belong to a union:** Gosia Wozniacka, "Less than 1 Percent of US Farmworkers Belong to a Union. Here's Why," *Civil Eats,* May 7, 2019, https://civileats.com/2019/05/07/less-than-1-percent-of-us-farmworkers-belong-to-a-union-heres-why/.

18 **Lupe enrolled in the second phase:** Immigration documents and the fam-

ily's recollections indicate that Lupe likely got his green card during the second phase of Reagan's amnesty program, which applied to farmworkers. Lalo and Jaime, however, did not, and by the time the family set about applying for Jaime's green card, Lalo had already been convicted of two felonies and was no longer eligible.

18   **showed "good moral character":** What does "good moral character" mean in a legal context? According to U.S. Citizen and Immigration Services, a person can prove they have "good moral character" through family ties, lack of criminal history, education, employment history, law-abiding behavior such as paying taxes, community involvement, length of time in the U.S., and credibility. See https://www.uscis.gov/policy-manual/volume-12-part -f-chapter-2.

Chapter Two: Escoffier Reincarnate

23   **Lalo's twelfth year marked a sea change:** This is an estimate based on the timeline the family recalls.

23   **graduated from high school with a certificate in accounting:** It's common in Mexico for high school students to graduate with a certificate in a particular area that's sufficient to get an entry-level job.

27   **Jim Crow laws and the racist legacy that persisted:** Helen B. Marrow, "Race and the New Southern Migration, 1986 to Present," in *Beyond la Frontera: The History of U.S.–Mexico Migration*, edited by Mark Overmyer-Velázquez (Oxford: Oxford University Press, 2011).

27   **plentiful jobs, changing immigration policy, and inexpensive housing:** Mary E. Odem and Elaine Lacy, eds., *Latino Immigrants and the Transformation of the U.S. South* (Athens, GA: University of Georgia Press, 2009).

31   **Food is mentioned often:** For more on the history of the food of the Americas, see Sophie D. Coe, *America's First Cuisines* (Austin: University of Texas Press, 1994). And in Mexico, specifically, see Jeffrey M. Pilcher, *¡Que Vivan los Tamales! Food and the Making of Mexican Identity* (Albuquerque: University of New Mexico Press, 1998). And in Spanish, the excellent compilation coordinated by Janet Long, *Conquista y Comida: Consecuencias del encuentro de dos mundos* (Mexico City: Universidad Nacional Autónoma de México, 2018).

32   **1 to 2 percent of those at battle were Spanish:** Andrés Reséndez, "500 years after Aztec Rule, Mexico confronts a complicated anniversary," *National Geographic*, August, 21, 2021. This particular detail, the percentage of Spaniards at the battle, was sourced from Matthew Restall, *When Moctezuma Met Cortez: The Meeting that Changed History* (New York: Ecco, 2018).

33   **The introduction of pork was the most significant alteration:** Long, *Conquista y Comida*.

39   **Ripert introduced him to the dining room:** According to Lalo's memory.
Ripert declined to be interviewed.

Chapter Three: Mustang

46   **the cashier, Jung Ho Kim, refused:** Attempts to locate and interview Jung
Ho Kim were not successful.

46   **They pistol-whipped him in the forehead:** This section is based on wit-
ness and detective statements, taken together with Lalo's recollection of
events. Lalo does not wish to publicly reveal the identities of his accomplices.
Administrators at the DeKalb County Courthouse were unable to locate the
case file (area attorneys confirmed this was not unusual given the timeframe
and nature of the case), though Lalo shared some copies of court records.
The Chamblee police department was able to provide their file on the case,
though an administrator said that none of the officers who worked on it were
still on the police force, more than two decades later and efforts to locate
them were unsuccessful.

Chapter Four: Ramen with Doritos

50   **Frank Scott State Prison in Hardwick, Georgia:** This facility was originally
built as a mental hospital and converted into a prison in 1975. It closed in
2009, when it was deemed an inefficient prison to operate due to a lack of
safety features. Daniel McDonald, "Another Prison Gone," *Union–Recorder*
(Milledgeville, GA), July 8, 2009, https://www.unionrecorder.com/archives/
another-prison-gone/article_43c794db-932a-5007-9d02-b4b3d088993b
.html.

51   **work out a plea deal:** Gonzalez did not recollect Lalo's case and could not
confirm the terms of his plea bargain. "I'm sorry," she said, "Twenty years ago,
thousands of cases." She no longer had his case file.

51   **sentenced to three years minus the eight months he'd served:** It's unclear
if Lalo's sentence was three years or four years, minus the eight months in
county jail, but information in the Georgia inmate database indicates that
three years is more likely.

53   **an administrative process:** According to immigration attorneys familiar with procedure for incarcerated individuals, this is normal practice, an
administrative action that can result in their transfer to a different facility.

56   **Natalia called with grave news:** Memories of this interval are unclear. They
range from a few weeks to a couple of months.

Chapter Five: The Golden Cage

60   **"La Jaula de Oro":** The song was written by Sinaloan singer Enrique Franco
Aguilar. You can watch Los Tigres del Norte perform it at Folsom Prison
here: https://www.youtube.com/watch?v=BnvNfE9fOv4.

60 **By then, Lalo had fallen in love:** Several unsuccessful attempts were made to contact and interview Max's mother. Lalo's family has also been unsuccessful in their attempts to contact her over the years.

61 **a style dubbed molecular gastronomy:** The term was coined by chemists Nicholas Kurti and Hervé This in 1988. Ferran Adrià of El Bulli became its most famous practitioner; El Bulli closed in 2011. For a narrative treatment of the movement, see John Lanchester, "Incredible Edibles," *New Yorker*, May 21, 2011.

Chapter Six: The Return

74 **plate of foie gras and black truffles:** "Entrevista Con Enrique Olvera," *Time Out Mexico*, June 14, 2012.

78 **As Olvera put it, "I can't think of a restaurant as shitty today":** It's worth reading Ruvalcaba's entertaining treatment of Pujol's evolution, along with more of Olvera's colorful quotes, in the retrospective volume *Pujol Veinte* (Mexico City: Culinary S.A. de C.V., 2020).

79 **a piece by *Texas Monthly* food critic Patricia Sharpe:** Sharpe also points out two earlier examples of the slow process of integrating Mexican food into fine dining spaces: Rosa Margarita Martin of Estoril, and Arnulfo Luengas, the corporate chef of the Banco Nacional de México. Patricia Sharpe, "Mix Masters," *Texas Monthly*, June 1991, https://www.texasmonthly.com/food/mix-masters/.

80 **performing class difference:** As Pilcher writes, hierarchies linked to food preceded the conquest among Mesoamerican peoples: nobility had more access to animal protein, and the Mexica condescended to groups that "ate leftovers," "cooked with neither skill nor sanitation," or "supposedly picked their corn before it ripened." While the responsibilities of the kitchen have historically burdened women across cultures, the extraordinarily physical and time-consuming effort to make tortillas is especially notable, at one time requiring "as much as a third of a woman's waking life." Jeffrey M. Pilcher, *¡Que Vivan los Tamales! Food and the Making of Mexican Identity* (Albuquerque: University of New Mexico Press, 1998).

81 **move away from a way of life:** David S. Dalton, *Mestizo Modernity: Race, Technology, and the Body in Postrevolutionary Mexico* (Gainsville: University of Florida Press, 2018).

82 **1831 Mexican recipe book *El Cocinero Mexicano*:** Subsequent editions of this anonymous cookbook remain in print. See Cristina Barros, *El cocinero Mexicano: México, 1831* (Mexico City: Dirección General de Culturas Populares, 2000).

82 **cataloguing these recipes homogenized the food itself:** S. B. G. Corona, "French-Fashioned Mexican Recipe Books in the 19th Century: Globalization and Construction of a National Culinary Model," *Anthropology of Food* S6 (2009).

83   **earthquake can be amplified by as much as one hundred times:** For more
      on the science behind Mexico City's earthquakes, and seismologist Lucy
      Jones of the U.S. Geological Survey, see Laura Tillman and Rong-Gong Lin
      II, "Mexico City residents whose buildings survived the 1985 quake thought
      they'd be safe in the next big one. They were wrong," *Los Angeles Times*, Sep-
      tember 20, 2017.

83   **kidnapping of Alfredo Harp Helú:** Associated Press, "Mexican Banker's
      Family Agrees to Pay Ransom," *Los Angeles Times*, June 25, 1994.

90   **became a significant recipient of enslaved Africans:** Douglas Richmond,
      "The Legacy of African Slavery in Colonial Mexico, 1519–1910," *Journal of
      Popular Culture* 35, no. 2 (March 5, 2004), https://onlinelibrary.wiley.com/
      doi/abs/10.1111/j.0022-3840.2001.00001.x.

91   **the consumption of ants:** As chef Ricardo Arellano of Oaxaca's Criollo told
      a reporter, "When a mother is trying to feed her family and there is no food,
      these ants are a good option because they have a rich flavor and are high in pro-
      tein." Susannah Rigg, "A Sauce Made from Flying Ants," BBC, June 9, 2017,
      https://www.bbc.com/travel/article/20170608-a-sauce-made-from-flying
      -ants.

      Chapter Seven: Máximo Bistrot Local

98   *Me queda claro que para pendejo no se estudia*: Literally, this translates to
      "it's clear to me that to be an idiot you don't have to study," but "clearly, some
      people are born idiots" is the most similar expression in English.

111   **even the world:** La Liste, which ranks international restaurants, has named
      Le Bernardin the top restaurant in the world multiple times.

112   **a more recent invention:** The first celebrity chef was Alexis Soyer, born
      in France in 1810. While a few chefs were widely known before Soyer's
      appearance (for example, James Hemings, enslaved by Thomas Jefferson,
      who trained in French technique on a 1784 trip to Paris and helped popu-
      larize dishes like macaroni and cheese and crème brûlée upon his return;
      Bartolomeo Scappi, the personal chef for several popes who authored the
      Renaissance cookbook *Opera* in the fifteenth century; and Guillaume Tirel,
      a fourteenth-century French court cook who wrote an influential cookbook
      of medieval recipes), Soyer's reputation far exceeded that of his predecessors.
      As Ruth Cowen writes, Soyer was "the first to understand the importance of
      nurturing a public profile, which he did through a combination of brilliant
      self-publicity and shameless press manipulation." Ruth Cowen, *Relish: The
      Extraordinary Life of Alexis Soyer, Victorian Celebrity Chef* (London: Weiden-
      feld and Nicolson, 2006).

113   **Chepina Peralta and Yuri de Gortari Krauss were go-to figures:** Going
      back even further, as Jeffrey Pilcher writes in *¡Que Viven los Tamales! Food
      and the Making of Mexican Identity* (Albuquerque: University of New Mexico

Press, 1998), "Clementina Cerrilla and Stella de Gamboa, home economics teachers in Mexico City, featured urban middle-class cuisine in cooking
shows in the 1920s and 1930s, but failed to reach a broad rural audience simply because at that early date few villages had radios." Other forces in the preservation and celebration of Mexico's food include Ricardo Muñoz Zurita, the
chef and restaurateur of Azul, British cookbook author Diana Kennedy, who
passed away in 2022, and chef Martha Ortiz of Dulce Patria.

113　**Yuri de Gortari Krauss, who led a movement:** Yuri de Gortari Krauss was
kind enough to participate in an interview for this book the year before his
death. He was dubious of the term *alta cocina* or haute cuisine, which he
felt referred more to class than quality of food. (*"Me parece una payasada,"*
he said; "I think it's a farce.") *Alta* translates to high, after all. He did not
consider his groundbreaking restaurant La Bombilla to have been a part of
Mexico's fine dining scene.

119　**the possibilities of the tamal:** Yuri de Gortari Krauss spoke about tamales
this way: "I always mention that there is no cuisine in the world that has a
dish as varied as the tamal is in Mexico. The Mextlapique, which is a tamal
made with *charrales* (small fish), you could find in the Mercado Merced, but
it's a type of tamal that doesn't have even a gram of dough. They put the fresh
charrales in the corn husk, they add chile veins, and grill it over coals. And
that's absolutely pre-Hispanic. Tamales that I love to eat and cook? Eat more
than prepare: the pibil pollo, which is a baked tamal for Día de los Muertos in
the Yucatán peninsula. I like to make sweet tamales with butter." For further
reading on the history of tamales, see Pilcher, *¡Que Vivan los Tamales! Food
and the Making of Mexican Identity.*

208　**elite environments to "elevate" endangered foods:** Alyshia Gálvez's book
Eating NAFTA: Trade, Food Policies, and the Destruction of Mexico (Oakland:
University of California Press, 2018) helped shape the prism through which
I understand Lalo's journey through the food system and its geopolitical con-
text. It's a breathtaking work of scholarship.

120　**Sowing Life:** For more on this program, see Max de Haldevang, "How Mexico's Vast Tree-Planting Program Ended up Encouraging Deforestation,"
Bloomberg News, March 8, 2021, https://www.bloomberg.com/news/features
/2021-03-08/a-tree-planting-program-in-mexico-may-encourage-deforestation.

120　**quadrupled its exports of corn:** For more on the impact of the North
American Free Trade Agreement on the economics of corn, see Gálvez, *Eating NAFTA.*

121　**viewing corn with suspicion:** For more on historical attacks on the tortilla,
see Pilcher, *¡Que Vivan los Tamales!* and Rebecca Earle's *The Body of the Conquistador: Food, Race and the Colonial Experience in Spanish America, 1492–
1700* (Cambridge: Cambridge University Press, 2012).

123　**mezcal is rapidly becoming too costly:** According to industry experts, while distillates sold as mezcal can still be found for drastically lower prices—around $10 a liter when purchased informally from distillers in the Oaxacan countryside—mezcal made from pure agave costs at least $35 a liter, climbing to $100 or more depending on the brand.

123   **"It's very particular people who can be those 'pioneers' ":** Gálvez also discusses the figure of La Malinche, the most famous example of a cultural broker in Mexican history. Born in the Pacific coastal state of Veracruz around 1500, La Malinche—or Malinalli, Doña Marina, Malinal, or Malintzin, as she is called in different accounts—was allegedly sold to traders after her father, a nobleman, died. As an enslaved person, she learned Maya dialects in addition to her native Nahuatl. After she was given to Hernán Cortés, along with nineteen other women, she became his principal interpreter, speaking Nahuatl, Maya, and Spanish. They also had a child together. Her work as an interpreter and negotiator became a crucial tool in Spain's dominance of the Aztec people, and her relationship with Cortés was regarded as traitorous. La Malinche's legacy is tinged with contempt. In *La Malinche in Mexican Literature: From History to Myth* (Austin: University of Texas Press, 1991), Sandra Messinger Cypess writes, "the one who conforms to her paradigm is labeled *malinchista*, the individual who sells out to the foreigner, who devalues national identity in favor of imported benefits." Scholars continue to attempt to parse her role in the conquest, and her position as both an interlocutor whose ability to alter the nature of communications between the Aztecs and Cortés gave her unique power, and as an enslaved person. Like so many indigenous people, La Malinche died of smallpox before reaching her thirtieth birthday.

Chapter Eight: Lady Profeco

129   **"What is this *pinche* fonda?":** Essentially, "What is this fucking diner?"

131   **the restaurant is the Chez Panisse of Mexico City:** Damien Cave, "Bad Reviews for Patron at Restaurant in Mexico," *New York Times*, April 29, 2013.

132   **#LadyProfeco became a meme:** "Lady" and "lord" have become a prefix for people who embody this phenomenon of privileged people behaving badly, using their status to shirk authority and/or accountability. Other examples include the Ladies de Polanco, a drunk pair of women who were videotaped insulting a police officer, and Lord Audi who was filmed when he rammed into a cyclist in a bike lane, told a cop to call his father, and then drove away from police. "*Esto es Mexico, güey*," he said during the interaction—"This is Mexico, dude."

133   **For Lalo, who worshipped Bourdain:** Bourdain once wrote: "Despite our ridiculously hypocritical attitudes towards immigration, we demand that Mexicans cook a large percentage of the food we eat, grow the ingredients we need to make that food, clean our houses, mow our lawns, wash our dishes, look after our children. As any chef will tell you, our entire service economy—the

restaurant business as we know it—in most American cities, would collapse overnight without Mexican workers. Some, of course, like to claim that Mexicans are 'stealing American jobs.' But in two decades as a chef and employer, I never had ONE American kid walk in my door and apply for a dishwashing job, a porter's position—or even a job as prep cook. Mexicans do much of the work in this country that Americans, probably, simply won't do. In nearly thirty years of cooking professionally, just about every time I walked into a new kitchen, it was a Mexican guy who looked after me, had my back, showed me what was what, was there—and on the case—when the cooks more like me, with backgrounds like mine—ran away to go skiing or surfing—or simply flaked."

136   **committed suicide by jumping from an international bridge:** Guadalupe Olivas Valencia died on February 17, 2017, an hour after being denied entry to the United States, where he had worked as a gardener for years. He had three children and was forty-four years old. Mexican media reported that he was distressed about returning to Mexico, and family members offered two explanations: that he was facing problems in Mexico and trying to get to the U.S. to escape them, or that he was desperate to find work to support his children. His wife had died three years earlier. He had previously been deported from the United States. Kate Linthicum, "Did a Mexican migrant leap to his death at the border minutes after deportation?," *Los Angeles Times*, February 22, 2017; Samantha Schmidt, "Moments after he was deported, a Mexican man jumped to his death off a border bridge, authorities believe," *Washington Post*, February 23, 2017.

Chapter Nine: El Jefe

141   **Brillat-Savarin's *The Physiology of Taste*:** Other memorable quotes: "The pleasure of the table belongs to all ages, to all conditions, to all countries, and to all areas. It mingles with all other pleasures, and remains at last to console us for their departure," and "Whoever receives friends and does not participate in the preparation of their meal does not deserve to have friends."

145   **That was only an illusion:** In the words of chef Marco Pierre White, "We live in a world of refinement, not invention."

Chapter Ten: Home

166   **most violent year on record:** "En 2018, la CDMX tuvo la tasa de homicidios más alta desde que se tiene registro," *Expansión Política*, April 3, 2019, https://politica.expansion.mx/cdmx/2019/04/03/2018-ano-mas-violento-cdmx-del-que-se-tenga-registro.

167   **In 2019, 8,345 people disappeared in Mexico:** Lidia Arista, "2019, el año con más desapariciones en México, reconoce Encinas," *Expansión Política*, October 7, 2020, https://politica.expansion.mx/mexico/2020/10/07/2019-el-ano-con-mas-desapariciones-en-mexico-reconoce-encinas.

Epilogue: Notes on a Plague

182 **this *bichito*:** Many in Mexico would refer to Covid-19 as the *bichito*, or little bug.

182 **Nearly 15,000 deaths:** Julia Hollingsworth, Jenni Marsh, Rob Picheta, Fernando Alfonso III, and Amir Vera, "March 22 Coronavirus News." CNN, March 22, 2020, https://edition.cnn.com/world/live-news/coronavirus -outbreak-03-22-20/index.html.

184 **13,000 shuttered:** Kate Linthicum, "COVID-19 is crushing Mexico City's food scene and the culinary energy that has made it so thrilling," *Los Angeles Times,* January 20, 2021.

185 **a coronavirus hotspot:** Alexis Triboulard and Mark Stevenson, "Latin America's Critical Food Markets Fuel Virus Spread," Associated Press, June 26, 2020, https://apnews.com/article/caribbean-peru-ap-top-news -venezuela-public-health-1bddc4345a272a919ce834e137a767ac.

185 **workers now being called "essential" would be forgotten:** Scarlett Lindeman, a restaurateur in Mexico City, wrote movingly about the inequalities the pandemic laid bare in an essay for *Hoja Santa* magazine. Everyone, she wrote, needs to eat during quarantine, "but the difference is evident in who has the luxury of staying at home, ordering dinner from UberEats and DiDi from people who make contactless delivery possible, by stocking the shelves at Sumesa and picking the limes in the fields." Scarlett Lindeman, "Y a ustedes, ¿Cómo les han tratado estos meses?," *Hoja Santa,* July 2021.

185 **130,000 Mexican children woke up:** "México es el país con mas huérfanos por COVID-19, según estudio," CNN Español, July 25, 2021, https://cnnespanol .cnn.com/2021/07/25/mexico-pais-con-mas-huerfanos-por-covid-19-segun -estudio-orix/.

186 **before a worker saw her day in court:** According to labor attorney Roberto Cruz Peña, the support system in Mexico for workers is the family. That serves to deepen inequality, with poor workers having no safety net whatsoever.

190 **Monsanto's weed killer Roundup:** This association is detailed in Paul J. Mills, Cyrielle Caussy, and Rohit Loomba, "Glyphosate Excretion Is Associated with Steatohepatitis and Advanced Liver Fibrosis in Patients With Fatty Liver Disease," *Clinical Gastroenterology and Hepatology* 18, no. 3 (2020): 741–43.

193 **blank sheets of paper:** According to labor attorney Roberto Cruz Peña, this is a common practice in Mexico. By forging a letter of resignation, an employer can skirt their obligations to pay severance when they fire an employee.

193 **anonymous accusations:** The group Terror Restaurants México began publicizing accusations and testimonials of labor abuse against the country's restaurants on its Instagram page in May of 2021. The group also maintains a

spreadsheet in which workers can anonymously log their accusations. As of this writing, 345 restaurants have been denounced there.

194 **street carts, stands, and fondas:** Lalo doesn't consume a great deal of street food, though many of the dishes sold by street vendors, like quesadillas, carnitas, and tamales, factored heavily in the development of his palate via Natalia's table. You can learn more about Mexico City's dizzying street food scene in Alonso Ruvalcaba's *24 horas de Comida en la Ciudad de Mexico* (Mexico City: Planeta, 2018), Lesley Téllez's cookbook *Eat Mexico: Recipes from Mexico City's Streets, Markets and Fondas* (London: Kyle Books, 2015), the food magazine *Hoja Santa*, available in English and Spanish, the whimsical Netflix series *Taco Chronicles*, and Lydia Carey's illustrated guidebook, *Mexico City Streets: La Roma* (Mexico City: Penguin Random House, 2018).

BIBLIOGRAPHY

Arellano, Gustavo. *Taco USA: How Mexican Food Conquered America*. New York: Scribner, 2012.

——."When the U.S. Government Tried to Replace Braceros with High Schoolers." NPR, August 23, 2018. https://www.npr.org/sections/thesalt/2018/07/31/634442195/when-the-u-s-government-tried-to-replace-migrant-farmworkers-with-high-schoolers.

Arista, Lidia. "2019, el año con más desapariciones en México, reconoce Encinas." *Expansión Política*, October 7, 2020. https://politica.expansion.mx/mexico/2020/10/07/2019-el-ano-con-mas-desapariciones-en-mexico-reconoce-encinas.

Ashabranner, Brent. *Dark Harvest: Migrant Farmworkers in America*. North Haven, CT: Linnet Books, 1993.

Bak-Geller Corona, Sarah. "Culinary Myths of the Mexican Nation." In *Cooking Cultures: Convergent Histories of Food and Feeding, Part IV – Food, Myth and Nostalgia*, edited by Ishita Banerjee-Dube. Cambridge: Cambridge University Press, 2016.

——. "French-fashioned Mexican recipe books in the 19th century: Globalization and construction of a national culinary model." *Anthropology of Food* S6 (2009).

Bardacke, Frank. "The UFW and the Undocumented." *International Labor and Working-Class History* 83, Special Issue: Strikes and Social Conflicts (2013): 162–69.

Barros, Cristina. *El cocinero Mexicano: México, 1831*. Mexico City: Dirección de Culturas Populares, 2000.

Bourdain, Anthony. *Kitchen Confidential: Adventures in the Culinary Underbelly*. New York: Ecco, 2000.

Cave, Damien. "Bad Reviews for Patron at Restaurant in Mexico." *New York Times*, April 29, 2013.

Clemens, Michael A., Ethan G. Lewis, and Hannah M. Postel. "Immigration Restrictions as Active Labor Market Policy: Evidence from the Mexican Bracero Exclusion." *American Economic Review* 108, no. 6 (2017): 1468–87.

Coe, Sophie D. *America's First Cuisines*. Austin: University of Texas Press, 1994.

Coerver, Don M., Suzanne B. Pasztor, and Robert Buffington. *Mexico: An Encyclopedia of Contemporary Culture and History*. Santa Barbara, CA: ABC CLIO, 2004.

Cortés, Hernán. *Hernán Cortés: Letters from Mexico*. Translated by Anthony Pagden. New Haven: Yale University Press, 2001.

Cowen, Ruth. *Relish: The Extraordinary Life of Alexis Soyer, Victorian Celebrity Chef*. London: Weidenfeld and Nicolson, 2006.

Cummins, Thomas B. F. Review of *Casta Paintings: Images of Race in Eighteenth-Century Mexico* by Ilona Katzew and *Imagining Identity in New Spain: Race, Lineage, and the Colonial Body in Portraiture and Casta Paintings* by Magali M. Carrera. *Art Bulletin* 88, no. 1 (2006): 185–89.

Dalton, David S. *Mestizo Modernity: Race, Technology, and the Body in Postrevolutionary Mexico*. Gainesville: University of Florida Press, 2018.

de Haldevang, Max. "How Mexico's Vast Tree-Planting Program Ended up Encouraging Deforestation." *Bloomberg News*, March 8, 2021.

Dubofsky, Melvyn. "Labor Unrest in the United States, 1906–90." *Review (Fernand Braudel Center)* 18, no. 1 (1995): 125–35.

Durand, Jorge, Jorge A. Schiavon, Patricia Arias, Nuty Cárdenas Alaminos, Mónica Jacobo, Diego Terán, and Miguel Vilches Hinojosa. *El Fenómeno Migratorio en Guanajuato: Diagnóstico y propuestas de política pública*. Mexico City: Secretaría del Migrante y Enlace Internacional, November 30, 2019, https://www.cide.edu/transparencia/fracciones/DOCUMENTOMIGRACIONGUANAJUATO.pdf.

Earle, Rebecca. *The Body of the Conquistador: Food, Race and the Colonial Experience in Spanish America, 1492–1700*. Cambridge: Cambridge University Press, 2012.

Ehrenreich, Barbara. *Nickel and Dimed: On (Not) Getting By In America.* New York: Henry Holt, 2002.

Escalante-Gonzalbo, Pablo, Bernardo García Martínez, Luis Jáuregui, Josefina Zoraida Vázquez, Elisa Speckman Guerra, Javier Garciadiego, and Luis Aboites Aguilar. *A New Compact History of Mexico.* Mexico City: El Colegio de Mexico, 2013.

Escoffier, Auguste. *Auguste Escoffier: Memories of My Life.* Translated by Laurence Escoffier. New York: Van Nostrand Reinhold, 1997.

Flores, Lori A. *Grounds for Dreaming: Mexican Americans, Mexican Immigrants, and the California Farmworker Movement.* New Haven and London: Yale University Press, 2016.

———. "A Town Full of Dead Mexicans: The Salinas Valley Tragedy of 1963, The End of the Bracero Program, and the Evolution of the Chicano Movement." *Western Historical Quarterly* 44, no. 2 (2013): 124–43.

Gálvez, Alyshia. *Eating NAFTA: Trade, Food Policies, and the Destruction of Mexico.* Oakland: University of California Press, 2018.

Grandin, Greg. *The End of the Myth: From the Frontier to the Border Wall in the Mind of America.* New York: Metropolitan Books, 2019.

Guérin-Gonzales, Camille. *Mexican Workers and American Dreams: Immigration, Repatriation, and California Farm Labor, 1900–1939.* New Brunswick, NJ: Rutgers University Press, 1994.

Guillermoprieto, Alma. *Looking at History: Dispatches from Latin America.* New York: Pantheon, 2001.

Haley, Andrew P. "The Nation Before Taste: The Challenges of American Culinary History." *Public Historian* 34, no. 2 (2012): 53–78.

Hamilton, Gabrielle. *Blood, Bones and Butter: The Inadvertent Education of a Reluctant Chef.* New York: Random House, 2011.

Harvest of Loneliness (Cosecha Triste). Film directed by Gilbert Gonzalez, Vivian Price, and Adrian Salinas. New York: Films Media Group, 2010.

Hentoff, Nat. "Cracking Heads in Georgia." *Washington Post,* June 14, 1997.

Holmes, Seth M. *Fresh Fruit, Broken Bodies: Migrant Farmworkers in the United States.* Berkeley: University of California Press, 2013.

Lander, Nicholas. *The Art of the Restaurateur.* New York: Phaidon, 2012.

Long, Janet, coordinator. *Conquista y Comida: Consecuencias del encuentro de dos mundos.* Mexico City: Universidad Nacional Autónoma de México, 2018.

Loza, Mireya. *Defiant Braceros: How Migrant Workers Fought for Racial, Sexual, and Political Freedom.* Chapel Hill: University of North Carolina Press, 2016.

Marrow, Helen B. "Race and the New Southern Migration, 1986 to Present." In *Beyond la Frontera: The History of U.S.–Mexico Migration,* edited by Mark Overmyer-Velázquez. Oxford: Oxford University Press, 2011.

McDonald, Daniel. "Another Prison Gone." *Union–Recorder* (Milledgeville, GA), July 8, 2009.

Meyer, Danny. *Setting the Table: The Transforming Power of Hospitality in Business.* New York: Harper, 2006.

Mills, Paul J., Cyrielle Caussy, and Rohit Loomba. "Glyphosate Excretion Is Associated with Steatohepatitis and Advanced Liver Fibrosis in Patients With Fatty Liver Disease." *Clinical Gastroenterology and Hepatology* 18, no. 3 (2020): 741–43.

Minian, Ana Raquel. *Undocumented Lives: The Untold Story of Mexican Migration.* Cambridge, MA: Harvard University Press, 2018.

Moore, Truman E. *The Slaves We Rent* New York: Random House, 1965.

Odem, Mary E., and Elaine Lacy, eds. *Latino Immigrants and the Transformation of the U.S. South.* Athens, GA: University of Georgia Press, 2009.

Perea, Juan F. "The Echoes of Slavery: Recognizing the Racist Origins of the Agricultural and Domestic Worker Exclusion from the National Labor Relations Act." *Ohio State Law Journal* 72, no. 1 (2011): 95–138.

Pilcher, Jeffrey M. *Planet Taco: A Global History of Mexican Food.* Oxford: Oxford University Press, 2012.

———. *¡Que Vivan los Tamales! Food and the Making of Mexican Identity.* Albuquerque: University of New Mexico Press, 1998.

Reséndez, Andrés. "500 years after Aztec rule, Mexico confronts a complicated anniversary." *National Geographic,* August 12, 2021.

Rozman Clark, Tea, Darlene Xiomara Rodriguez, and Lara Smith-Sitton. *Green Card Youth Voices: Immigration Stories from an Atlanta High School.* Minneapolis: Wise Ink Creative Publishing, 2018.

Ruvalcaba, Alonso. "Pujol: Twenty Years of Chilango Cuisine." In *Pujol Veinte.* Mexico City: Culinary S.A. de C.V., 2020.

Shallcross Koziara, Karen. "The Agricultural Minimum Wage: A Preliminary Look." *Monthly Labor Review* 90, no. 9 (1967): 26–29.

Sharpe, Patricia. "Mix Masters." *Texas Monthly*, June 1991. https://www
.texasmonthly.com/food/mix-masters/.

Vásquez-Medina, José Antonio. *Cocina, Nostalgia y Etnicidad: En Restaurantes
Mexicanos de Estados Unidos*. Barcelona: Editorial UOC, 2016.

Wilson, Eli Revelle Yano. *Front of the House, Back of the House: Race and Inequality in the Lives of Restaurant Workers*. New York: New York University Press,
2021.

Wozniacka, Gosia. "Less than 1 percent of farmworkers belong to a union.
Here's why." *Civil Eats*, May 9, 2019. https://civileats.com/2019/05/07/less
-than-1-percent-of-us-farmworkers-belong-to-a-union-heres-why/.

INDEX